"In a society where 'fixing' your negative body image requires changing your body, Greer provides a fresh biblical perspective to combat enslavement to this quick-fix, image obsessed, perfect body cultural ideology and helps you experience the true freedom of seeing your body as God does. This book is a must-read for parents, counselors, and teachers."

Pamela Cubas, Biblical Counselor,
Gospel Care Collective

"Miles. Calories. Gains. Restrictions. Indulgences. Heavy. Thin. Broken. Ruined. Can we even count the ways our relationship with our bodies may become unhealthy? *Struggling with Body Image* helps us take honest inventory of how we think of ourselves and points us to God's ever-needed grace and help."

Nate Brooks, Associate Professor of Counseling,
Southeastern Baptist Theological Seminary; founder,
Courage Christian Counseling

"Lainey Greer is both an expert on human embodiment and an author who winsomely addresses this critical topic. Most people at some time in their life wrestle with poor body image, and Lainey's book will help Christians see themselves truly as God sees them. If you struggle with body image or know someone who does, this book is for you!"

Gregg R. Allison, Professor of Christian Theology,
The Southern Baptist Theological Seminary; secretary,
Evangelical Theological Society; senior fellow for
gender and sexuality, Ethics and Religious Liberty
Commission; author of *Embodied: Living as Whole
People in a Fractured World*

"As a counselor, I am incredibly grateful for this book. Lainey sheds necessary light on the complexity of a negative body image throughout the lifespan but rightly brings God's Word to bear directly on that complexity. She shows us how to care well for brothers and sisters who struggle with a negative body image. I highly recommend that any counselor read this book!"

Kristin L. Kellen, Associate Director of EdD Studies and Associate Professor of Biblical Counseling, Southeastern Baptist Theological Seminary

"Lainey winsomely offers a comprehensive cultural analysis and biblical exegesis related to body image. Her research addresses related issues from childhood to adulthood and deep reflections on the body and soul. Most importantly, her Scriptural principles counteract the evil in and around us so that we can honor God with our bodies. Her book is a must-read!"

Robert K. Cheong, Founder and Executive Director, Gospel Care Ministries; author of *Restoration Story: Why Jesus Matters in a Broken World*

"Lainey Greer presents a helpful resource to understand body image and the significance of the body from a Christian perspective. Whether it's age-related changes, eating disorders, or the body positivity movement, Lainey challenges men and women, young and old, to glorify God with their bodies."

Lilly Park, Associate Professor of Biblical Counseling, Southwestern Baptist Theological Seminary

STRUGGLING WITH BODY IMAGE

SEEING WHAT GOD SEES

Lainey Greer

newgrowthpress.com

New Growth Press, Greensboro, NC 27401
newgrowthpress.com

Cover Template Design: Studio Gearbox, studiogearbox.com
Cover Art: Brad Hansen
Interior Typesetting/eBook: Lisa Parnell, lparnellbookservices.com

ISBN: 978-1-64507-452-6 (Print)
ISBN: 978-1-64507-453-3 (eBook)

Library of Congress Cataloging-in-Publication Data on file

Printed in the United States of America

31 30 29 28 27 26 25 24   1 2 3 4 5

CONTENTS

INTRODUCTION

For some people, body image is not a topic they spend much time considering. For others, a negative body image is a major impediment to their lives, plaguing their thoughts and interfering with their daily schedules. And then there are those few who are content with their bodies, whose body image is primarily healthy. No matter where you are on that spectrum, body image is an important topic—especially for Christians, who believe that God created our bodies and, in the incarnation, took one himself. But the body in general and body image specifically are seldom discussed in the church. How sad that such an important topic is often ignored, leaving Christians of all kinds of bodies trying to sort out their body image based on what they hear or see in popular culture!

This book aims to address this problem directly. After all, if God cares about the body, then *the way we see our bodies matter to him.* Because God calls his children to glorify him in the body (1 Corinthians 6:20), it is important to treat and think about the body in ways that honor him. Thus, body image—the way you think about or see your body—is of great consequence to the Christian faith.

So the goal of this book is to help believers develop a biblical understanding of the body that is foundational for a God-honoring body image. Everyone has a body image, and whether from popular culture stereotypes, social media, physical struggles, or age-related changes, most people battle a negative one. But because your body matters to God, it is important that his Word, and not the world, informs your body image.

The book will unfold in six chapters, beginning with an overall explanation of what body image is and why it matters. Next, we will consider where a negative body image comes from and then discuss the disordered responses that a negative body image can create. From there, the ways the world responds to a negative body image will be explained before looking at Scripture as the foundation for learning to see our bodies as God does. The book will wrap up with helping Christians think biblically about how to have a body image that honors God and helps us recognize the unique goodness of our bodies. This framework will then be applied to six case studies that represent common negative body image struggles for a disabled child, a teenage girl, a young adult, a postpartum mom, a menopausal woman, and a midseventies man.

This book is for those who personally struggle with negative body image, and also for those who want to help a loved one, or seek deeper understanding in order to advise those in your care. It will help you to hold a body image that honors God by seeing your body as he does, and it will help you to guide others to do the same. Reflection questions will also guide you to think about each chapter's content more deeply and apply it practically.

MY STORY

But before we get into those discussions, I want to share some of my body image struggles.

I remember feeling troubled by my body in elementary school. Always in the back row on picture day, I towered over classmates, including most of the boys. For years, my grandfather affectionately called me "hoss," while my grandmother explained that I was "big boned" like other family members. According to my mom, I was "stocky." You know that good kind of big-boned-stocky-hoss that every girl wants to be.

My hair was a combination of wavy and poofy, which meant it was totally unmanageable before the days of straighteners and curling wands. Thankfully, before sixth grade, my mom stopped crafting the biggest, bushiest bangs you ever saw, and braces corrected a massive front tooth gap. I am beyond grateful that Facebook did not exist in those days.

Amid all the awkward teenage body angst, a middle school boy heard that I liked him. To make matters worse, he glibly told my friend that he would not go out with me. His reason? I was too big to be a girl. With one passing comment, my fears about my big-boned, stocky frame were confirmed by an eleven-year-old, prepubescent boy.

Those mortifying days of middle school slowly morphed into high school where my body type was sought after for sports like basketball and softball. I used my hoss-like frame to box out and grab rebounds on the basketball court. In softball, my stature was an asset, as it increased my range, helping me to play first and third base. Though I was an athlete, I was still self-conscious about my body. My stomach was not exactly flat, and my hips were wide—so wide that I was mocked with an embarrassing nickname. To top it off, I also had a serious bike wreck that left large, noticeable scars on my knee, which people often mistook for dirt. So the discolored skin on my knee was a constant bother. The list could go on.

Thinking back over these "flaws" now sounds ridiculous. But in those formative years, I obsessed over them. I was uncomfortable and ashamed of my body. I realize now that my issues were like the struggles experienced by others, because nearly all of us—men and women, young and old—struggle with body image at some point.

After those formative years came years of change, growth, and preparation for the work I do now. It begin with a severe trial in my early twenties and a period of depression and anorexia which only added to my negative body image. During that time, I worked in church ministry and was a personal trainer where I mostly trained Christians. In those two seemingly divergent career paths, I recognized that many believers, including myself, failed to think about or treat their bodies well. Additionally, I discipled many young women who struggled in similar ways I once did. I was able to comfort others with the comfort God had given me in my own battles (2 Corinthians 1:3–4). So I became passionate about helping believers with two things: a growing understanding of theology and how to care for themselves physically.

With those emphases, I devoted my doctoral work to developing a theology of human embodiment that I applied to body image. In this focus, I could see the Lord bring together my two passions: theology and the body. So I worked on discerning a biblical view of how God sees our bodies, and connecting that to what it means to glorify him in our bodies (1 Corinthians 6:20). I believe glorifying God in our bodies plays out in two main ways: how we think about our bodies, or body image, and how we treat our bodies, or body stewardship. While this book is not about body stewardship, it is also an important subject for Christians to connect with a biblical view of the body, especially for those in ministry. Burnout is an unfortunate reality in our fast-paced society, but the added stress of serving others makes it essential to treat the body well. With my background in personal training and own experience with ministry burnout, some of my work focuses on helping believers steward their bodies in the areas of nutrition, exercise, rest, and stress management.

It is essential that Christians develop a theology of the body that can be a foundation for a healthy body image. In my doctoral work, I set out to develop a theology of the body based on 1 Corinthians 6:12–20. This passage will be discussed at greater length in chapter 6, where we will consider how Paul develops a trinitarian approach to body image in order to correct the way the Corinthians thought about their bodies, which led them to sin and dishonor God with their bodies. Throughout the book, but largely in that chapter, I use some of the content from my dissertation.

Paul's argument and its connection to the body has significant implications for body image. This book reflects my dissertation research, which aimed at laying a theological foundations for godly living. Once you finish the book, my prayer is that you will see the connection that Paul made to the Corinthians—that the command to glorify God in the body began with the call to think rightly about their bodies. In other words, God wants us to see our bodies the way he does.

So what about you? When you picture your body, does it measure up? Are you concerned about the size of your nose? What about a double chin that shows up when you move your head a certain way or your seemingly extra-long torso? When you forget to suck your stomach in, are you worried that others notice? How about your lack of muscle mass or short stature? How do you feel when you cannot wear a hat that covers your receding hairline? Or what about when your body limits you, keeping you from activities you once enjoyed with ease?

Because a negative body image can focus on a specific body part or the body's size and shape, the troubling issues are endless. Just about any physical feature can lead to a mental judgment about whether your body is good enough. If you conclude that it isn't, you begin to develop a negative body image. While some people might assess their bodies positively and others with indifference, most people suffer from negative body image. For that reason, this book will focus on negative body image (although there will be some discussion of body image in general), and then equip you with biblical tools that will help you build a God-honoring body image.

Chapter 1

WHAT IS BODY IMAGE AND WHY DOES IT MATTER?

Clay is starting college. Last season, his high school teammates teased him about being "too thin." He knew they were just kidding, but as he gets ready to meet new people, he can't get it out of his mind. He decides to make a plan to start lifting weights. Beginning college with a new, more muscular body would help him meet friends, even get a girlfriend. But looking through social media for the best weightlifters to follow begins to consume Clay's time. Finding the biggest guys, following their eating plans, and building the most effective lifting routines is all he focuses on. He's about to leave for college, but all he really cares about is achieving the perfect body before he gets there.

If you have ever looked in the mirror and reflected on what you saw, you might have had similar thoughts to Clay. How he thinks about his appearance is an important part of his body image. The same is true for all of us. Perhaps you've provided a description of your physical form to someone else. The bodily characteristics, flaws, or hang-ups you highlighted would be a good indicator of your body image. Or maybe you are noticing changes in your body's form or function, and these changes creep into your mind throughout the day. Perhaps you are troubled by your body image, even more than you realize.

Before we can address a negative body image, we first need to understand what body image is and how it develops. This chapter will define body image and trace its development as we age, so that we can identify challenges at various life stages. Finally, we will set body image in its proper context within a biblical worldview, which is a key step toward altering negative body image and seeing your body the way God sees it.

BODY IMAGE DEFINED

Body image has three components: a mental picture, subjective filter, and resulting assessment. First, body image involves a mental depiction of your physical form. Second, that mental picture gets passed through a self-defined, subjective framework or filter. Third, that biased filtering results in an assessment, and the outcome describes your body image.

Essentially, body image is the way you visualize your body. It is an internalized picture of your physical appearance that may or may not reflect reality. Usually, that mental picture is skewed because it gets passed through a framework that springs from internal, idealized standards that you set for yourself. When that framework leads you to judge your body as inadequate and unsatisfactory, your thoughts, emotions, and actions are influenced by the negative ways you assess your body. All of this is included in what we mean when we talk about negative body image.

But to see our bodies as God does, Christians need to switch out the middle component. Rather than passing the mental picture through a subjective framework that results in a harsh assessment, Christians can replace their framework with a biblical one. No matter the mental image we hold, as it passes through God's Word, we focus our minds on truth, regardless of the perceived flaws in our mental picture. Then, by depending on God's grace and choosing to agree with the way he sees our bodies, we release societal expectations that lead our minds and hearts away from truth to lies and negativity. In this way, once we exchange the filter, we can assess our body according to Scripture, which produces a God-honoring body image. Just as doing other things God's way is part of his good plans for us, so is viewing our bodies the way he does. As we move toward this goal, we need to learn about body image development.

BODY IMAGE DEVELOPMENT

Everyone has a body image because we are all embodied beings, living in a place and time, experiencing physical changes and external factors that influence our mental picture, subjective framework, and resulting assessment. The process of body image formation begins at a young age.

Body image in children

Bodily recognition and comparison occur in both boys and girls from our earliest years. In children twelve and under, body image steadily changes, beginning with infants who distinguish between themselves and other babies in pictures and videos. By age two, children refer to themselves in the first person and recognize their personal characteristics in the mirror. At four to five years, children start to assess and compare their appearance to others. If their body is different in weight, height, or disability, negative body image can form even then. By age six, children become preoccupied with their bodies in new ways, noticing things that cause dissatisfaction with their bodies. At eight years old, there is significant progression in evaluation and comparison, as children become aware of other factors that shape body image like achievements in school, the number of friends they have, their athletic ability or lack thereof, along with physical form.[1] From a young age, the three components of body image—mental picture, subjective framework, and resulting assessment—take shape, and many people feel displeasure over their physical appearance, even in their early, developmental years.

Many factors that influence body image in children are similar to those that affect adults. One factor that seems to have the greatest influence is body mass index (BMI), which is a ratio of height and weight. Higher weight results in a higher BMI. While an increased BMI often has a negative impact on body image in adults, it seems to be the main cause of negative body image in children. This is especially the case in the US, where childhood obesity impacts 1 in 5 children.[2] As children grow and perceive differences in themselves and others, they connect their self-worth to whether their bodies are like those of their peers.[3] Take boys ages six to eight as an example. One study found that 35 percent believe they should be thinner to achieve an ideal body. This is a hard thing for a first grader to feel.[4] This early formation of a negative body image can create a pattern of harmful thoughts and feelings that contributes to a poor body image for years to come.

Additionally, BMI can pose another threat to body image. If a child with a lower BMI assesses higher weight as something to avoid, this desire can manifest in a fixation on weight that may lead to body image disorders on down the road. Over 80 percent of ten-year-olds are reportedly afraid of being "fat," and this fear can drive extreme behaviors like diet obsession in order to actualize an idealized body image. With this idealized image already formed within the first decade of life, it comes as no surprise that 46 percent of nine-to-eleven-year-olds admit to regular dieting.[5]

While there are several factors that teach children body ideals, the most influential come from their social context—parents, media, teasing from siblings, or comparisons with their peers.[6] Given the rise of smart phones, social media has come to strongly influence body image formation, as a compilation of studies in seventeen countries have shown.[7] Early on, children gain awareness of appearance ideals from pictures that are shared on social media platforms. These posts give viewers a sense of what is a "good" or "bad" picture, which children typically connect to their self-worth. Seeing the number of likes or comments can further link their appearance to how they feel about themselves. Children learn that being called pretty or handsome in pictures is a good thing, which reinforces their own satisfaction.[8] In many ways, because of social media, children are often taught to care about their appearance at much younger ages than ever before. As parents and caregivers consider social media exposure in children, they should recognize that in 2023 the Surgeon General failed to "conclude that social media is sufficiently safe for children and adolescents."[9] Christians should avoid being uninformed about the implications of social media exposure, especially among children. Because it is such a challenging topic that requires wisdom and discernment, social media's impact on negative body image will be treated more fully in the next chapter.

Body image in adolescence

After childhood, body image development accelerates for teenagers. When you think about all the social, behavioral, and physical changes that occur in these years, it's easy to see how this is an essential period for body image development. While I will primarily address social media's influence on body image in the next chapter, it is important to recognize that many teens receive their own phones around this age. With a device for constant comparison in their hands, these years can dramatically heighten body image concerns. And, even without their own phone, a teen may appear in others' pictures, which are often "liked" and commented upon by others.

During adolescence, teens begin to listen to peers over parents and desire the body type and abilities of others. In the transition from elementary to middle school, teens frequently have to learn how to navigate new social settings, including new schools, friends, and teachers, on top of learning how to handle normal teenage angst. The desire to fit in socially increases during these years, perhaps more than at any other time in life. If fitting in means looking or dressing a certain way, negative body image can be exacerbated. Media weighs more on body image in adolescence primarily because a teen's exposure to new TV shows, movies, or social media access also increases in these years. Increased media exposure often promotes body image issues, with one study finding nearly 50 percent of adolescents between the ages of thirteen and seventeen report a worsening body image.[10]

For teenagers, whose emotions are often volatile, negative emotions are frequently linked to the way they view their bodies. To fit in, teens may begin to change their eating and exercising behaviors. To meet a physical ideal, boys might turn to spending hours in the gym, while girls restrict their food intake. These new behaviors, especially in the teenage years, can lay the foundation for an eating disorder or exercise obsession.

Puberty occurs during adolescence as well. If a teen's body begins to change sooner than others, it can create a negative body image. Think of the girl whose body has begun depositing fat in her hips before her friends. She might perceive these changes as unwanted weight gain without understanding that puberty began earlier for her than it did for others. Similarly, when a teenager's body fails to change as fast as his peers, negative body image can develop. Consider the thirteen-year-old boy whose friends have grown taller and more muscular than him. Comparison and dissatisfaction commonly occur when a teen perceives his or her body as inadequate or different from others in these years. While comparison still drives dissatisfaction in adults, age-related physical changes also play an important role in adults' body image development.

Body image in adults

Adults continue to face the pressure of societal body standards as they age. With age comes significant shifts in our bodies, such as weight variations from a slowing metabolism, pregnancy, or menopause, hearing and eyesight decline, skin wrinkles, hair loss, and muscle atrophy, along with general aches and pains that limit motion, balance, and normal everyday activities. When men and women struggle to balance shifting physical realities and appearance expectations, negative body image frequently results. While these struggles are understandable and common to most people, an increasing awareness of them can be a helpful recognition in the development of body image.

Most adult women report displeasure with their weight and body shape.[11] Typically, the same bodily areas that frustrate teenagers and young women still trouble older women, and weight gain remains a significant determiner of body image. Pregnancy and menopause most commonly contribute to higher weight, which highly impacts body image. Women who gain weight despite engaging in healthy eating and exercise habits can be especially frustrated and vulnerable to negative body image. As their body image develops, most women continue to compare themselves to others, which only serves to reinforce undue physical expectations. The process generally continues until elderly years when women display more realistic body expectations that are less dictated by cultural standards. This decrease in appearance issues comes with a lesser emphasis on temporal concerns and greater acceptance of current life stage.[12]

Compared to females, male body image is more difficult to determine as adult men are less inclined to admit body displeasure.[13] Though the majority of college-age men acknowledge a negative body image, it has commonly been accepted that fewer men struggle with negative body image than women.[14] However, men are also influenced by cultural ideals. For example, as men reach middle age, some articulate the ideal body as much slimmer than their current perception of themselves, which indicates a struggle with negative body image. Many men report a desire to rewind the clock and look like they did earlier in life.[15] Men also admit their body image worsened around age sixty, which differs from women. This change in body image often occurs when men began to desire their former, youthful body.[16] If men cannot alter expectations for their aging bodies, they can develop a negative body image, perhaps for the first time in their life.

UNDERSTANDING BODY IMAGE FROM A BIBLICAL PERSPECTIVE

The question for believers is, How should we think about our bodies? Is God really concerned with our thoughts, specifically our body image? Yes! Because he commands us to glorify him in our bodies (1 Corinthians 6:20), this instruction informs our actions and should include the thoughts we nurture about our physical frame. We need to recognize that a God-honoring body image falls within that command, a command that is meant to guide all thoughts and actions for our good. To develop a biblical framework that allows us to see our bodies the way God does, we need a theology of the body.

Very simply, a theology of the body recognizes the major ways that Scripture talks about the body and then organizes the Bible's teaching into clear themes. A theology of the body helps us understand how our bodies were made, how to value them, who they belong to, what they should do, and where they are going. All of these aspects are essential for truly seeing our bodies as God sees them. When we study what Scripture says about how our bodies were made, we find that you and I were created as God's embodied image-bearers, a fundamental reality that means God formed us as immaterial and material, soul and body beings. God designed us in his image as embodied men and women, whose souls and bodies are purposeful, full of dignity and value.

Let's look at some of the key passages of Scripture on which we can build a biblical foundation for how we view our bodies.

A BIBLICAL FOUNDATION FOR HOW TO VIEW OUR BODIES

In Genesis 1:26–28 we learn that God creates humans as soul and body beings, made in his image, as either male or female. Filled with value and dignity, we reflect God's image as embodied beings with physical and spiritual capacity to enjoy creation and be in relationship with our Creator. We need a body to fulfill his creation commands to be fruitful, multiply, and fill the earth. And through our physical senses, we experience the material world that declares his beauty and majesty. We also have a soul so we can personally know the One who created us for life with him.

Our birth as either male or female was miraculously planned according to God's perfect will. Though our culture might question or deny fundamental truths like biological sex, we hold fast to what God says about the body. We believe that our bodies bear his image and are purposefully made male or female. Because God declared the creation of his embodied image-bearers to be *very good*, then believers can embrace this remarkable declaration as the path to true flourishing.

In Psalm 139:13–16 we learn that just as wondrous creations in the natural world inspire worship and awe, so should the wondrous creation of our physical bodies. In these verses, David proclaims God's sovereign knowledge over his whole life—his thoughts, words, struggles, and every part of his body. As God is the Creator of all, so he created David's inward parts, knitting them together in his mother's womb. To knit requires time, intentionality, and care. David knows the work God did in constructing his body is praiseworthy. His intricately woven and stitched-together body was known by God before David came into being, a body through which he will live out the days God has written in his book. David marvels over and praises God for two things that he so wonderfully formed: his body and the days God planned for him to live out. These truths proclaim that nothing about your existence is accidental. Every part is integral to making you the person God created you to be to live out the life he planned for you.

In Acts 17:24–28, Paul confirms that God created each of us as an embodied being and has determined the exact time and place we will live. God wants the people of Athens (and us!) to know that God desires a relationship with his image-bearers and plans for our location and life circumstances to drive us to him. That means everything about your existence is within God's sovereign plans—your family, ethnicity, sex, disability, genetics, everything that makes you, you. These precise details are experienced through our bodies as we rely on God for our very life and breath. So we view our bodies through the lens of his providential plans worked out in a particular place and time with a specific physical makeup. Rather than being dissatisfied with our shape or form, we find reason to trust God's plans for when and how he created us. As we shift our focus to God's good plans, he will use every circumstance, including times of body dissatisfaction, to teach us that lasting satisfaction is found in him alone.

Recognizing the body as part of the image of God is a crucial component of seeing the body as God does. After all, if we fail to respect the body, then we will excuse all sorts of behaviors. If we dislike our bodies, we will be more likely to mistreat them. If the heart posture toward our bodies is one of disdain, it will be difficult to honor God in our body. These types of bodily conceptions will never provide a solid foundation for a God-honoring body image. Because God created us as embodied beings and commands us to glorify him in our bodies, surely we must conclude that the thoughts we entertain about our bodies matter to him. He desires that we see our bodies the same way he does.

REFLECTION QUESTIONS

1. How do you see your body?
2. Do you find body image a common struggle? If yes, can you recall how these struggles began?
3. How has your body image changed with age?
4. Why do Christians need to have a theology of the body?

Chapter 2

WHERE DOES NEGATIVE BODY IMAGE COME FROM?

Cynthia is married, in her sixties, and is blessed to spend lots of time with her grandkids. But she is never satisfied with what she sees in the mirror, especially after going through menopause. She thinks often about how doesn't want to look old or the feeling that she keeps "getting fatter." In fact, she's been comparing different cosmetic procedures to address the areas of concern. She has also started taking medication guaranteed to help her lose weight. Her friends are aware of her ongoing concerns and wonder what lengths she will go in her pursuit of a "better body."

Cynthia may sound extreme to you (or she may sound like lots of people you know), but most people will experience a negative body image at some point in their lives. Though commonly associated with teenage girls, the experience of negative body image is widespread, especially because of the influence of cultural expectations, aging-related changes, media, and relationships. Shifts in how we think and feel about our bodies are inevitable, but common, everyday occurrences can ramp up sinful thoughts and destructive emotions even more.

Throughout the day, you are confronted with numerous influences, and it can be hard to avoid ordinary things that prompt dissatisfaction with your physical appearance. For instance, each look in the mirror may tempt you to focus on some area of bodily concern. Or your peers can be another pressure point. And if you already dislike your body, these feelings compound if others tease about your appearance. For many people, social media can prompt dissatisfaction. Each scroll through social media presents an opportunity to find new ways your body fails to measure up. And of course, your own mind can be a frequent source of temptation. The cycle of negative thoughts and feelings about your body grows worse if you beat yourself up for the way you look. And then the culture plays its own part too. Confusing messages about what it means to be male or female devalue the body and can create or exacerbate body image issues. For Christians, we must guard against allowing these ordinary things to prompt us to form a negative body image. Being on guard against them begins with understanding them.

From cultural standards and personality tendencies to sports and media, we will look at a variety of contributors to negative body image in this chapter. But spoiler alert! Social media has become the biggest contributor and is continuing to increase its hold on the way we see our bodies. Before considering these contributors, we must define negative body image and differentiate it from body dysmorphic disorder before considering ways to assess how our view of the body affects us.

WHAT IS NEGATIVE BODY IMAGE?

As discussed in the previous chapter, body image relies on three components—a mental picture of the body, a subjective framework, and a resulting assessment. Negative body image is a perception of outward appearance that, when passed through a subjective framework, produces discontent when the body is assessed as lacking in some way. While you may entertain a mental picture of your entire body, negative body image can also focus on certain body parts. But it does not stop there. Holding unhelpful thoughts about your body can impact emotional well-being and lead to harmful actions that are intended to help you achieve whatever appearance ideals are driving your negative body image.

For Christians who struggle to see their bodies as God does, we need a new framework, one that stands between our mental picture and resulting judgment. When we can leave behind our self-defined, subjective framework for an objective one that rests on God's Word, we will be sufficiently equipped to deal with negative body image, tackle challenging emotions, and put a stop to harsh judgments and actions that do not glorify God.

While negative body image is not classified as a mental disorder, body dysmorphic disorder is and must be understood as distinct from body dissatisfaction.

BODY DYSMORPHIC DISORDER

Body dysmorphic disorder is a category of negative body image that exists on its own due to its extreme body mischaracterization, going far deeper than adverse thoughts and feelings. There are three main criteria. First, a person fixates on one or more perceived body "flaws," which are often imperceptible to others. Finding these areas repulsive, the sufferer focuses on them for hours a day. Second, because of this fixation, the sufferer engages in obsessive behaviors to address the issues. Behaviors include constant comparing, examining the flaws, excessive grooming, seeking reassurance, pursuing cosmetic surgery, overexercising, extreme tanning, and constantly changing clothes. Third, these behaviors interrupt normal functioning in everyday activities.[1] Though sufferers of body dysmorphic disorder should receive professional help, most cases go undiagnosed and without adequate treatment.[2]

Those with body dysmorphic disorder clearly experience a negative body image, and perhaps surprisingly, it affects men and women equally.[3] Given its extreme nature, its occurrence in both sexes, and its underdiagnosis, Christians need a growing awareness of it alongside negative body image. We must take care to not conflate the two or make light of the fixation and dysphoria that characterize the disorder.[4] While a biblical view of the body will help guide someone with body dysmorphic disorder, treatment might require considering medical interventions for major depression and suicidal ideation that can coincide with body dysmorphic disorder.[5]

CONTRIBUTING FACTORS

Negative body image triggers are plentiful, often causing dejected emotions and potentially damaging actions. Triggers vary from person to person and can come from social interactions, getting on a scale, walking in front of a mirror, eating, self-talk, exercising, getting dressed, media exposure, and more. The primary contributors to negative body image are social, behavioral, and physical. Social factors include cultural expectations, the influence of family and friends, and media. Behavioral elements that contribute to negative body image are personality tendencies, habits, self-talk, and patterns of sin in our thinking, feeling, and acting. Physically, several biological realities like genetics, puberty, weight, and aging each contribute to negative body image. We will consider these factors in detail.

Social Contributors

Social contributors to negative body image are all around us. Some are avoidable, like social media accounts that trigger harmful body thoughts or a movie that produces unreasonable expectations. Others may be more difficult to prevent, like shifting cultural expectations on what an acceptable body looks like or a family member's conscious, and even subconscious, influence. Still, building an awareness of these triggers can help to protect against negative body image issues.

Cultural expectations

Every culture imparts its own messages that form the way people perceive they should behave, look, or feel. These messages are absorbed daily and become the standard to which people compare themselves. Often, if we find ourselves failing to meet societal ideals, feelings of insufficiency follow. This common response can result in a negative body image.

One such message is what the "perfect" female body looks like. Amazingly, according to the average American, acceptable proportions for women are having a 26-inch waist, being five feet five inches tall, and weighing 128 pounds.[6] The trouble is these proportions are nearly unattainable apart from unhealthy endeavors, a reality that fails to influence these expectations. How is it possible for women not to battle negative body image when this is the expectation?

These cultural messages then combine with cultural norms designed to achieve that ideal figure. Extreme exercise, radical diet plans, plastic surgeries, steroids, body-shaping procedures, and weight loss pills are various ways we are encouraged to try to reach that ideal body. According to the culture, nothing lies outside the realm of possibility when it comes to sculpting the "right" body. And let's be clear. There is an unlimited profit to be made in the health and fitness industry, so it is not shocking that we are inundated with messages meant to drive us toward pills or products to fix a negative body image. But on top of the financial investment this commitment requires, it often comes at a cost to physical health.

Thinness and muscularity reign as the prevailing cultural ideals in the West. With skinny as the marker of beauty in women and bulky as the expectation for men, the culture says again and again to those who already feel inadequate that, yes, they are inferior compared to those with the proper proportions or abilities. Because these ideals are pushed through models, media, digital images, and advertising, they serve as regular triggers for negative body image. And children are not immune to these messages either. Weeding out these toxic messages and replacing them with biblical truths should be a priority for believers of all ages.

Family and friends

Whether intentionally or unintentionally, family and friends perpetuate societal standards that can greatly impact others. While various kinds of media play a role, we also learn these standards from those around us. Body image is often tied to familial influence, whether by directly talking about appearance or indirectly setting an example of bodily concern.[7] Regular comments from a parent about their child's weight or physique can influence negative body image. Teasing from a sibling may quickly contribute to feelings of bodily dissatisfaction. Or a family member's obsession with dieting or bodybuilding can model and pass on that same concern to others.

As for the influence of friends, females tend to build friendships based on similar body image or dietary concerns. Males form friendships in much the same way, as both males and females are highly influenced by others' expectations and comments.[8] When ridicule is involved, those comments are especially lasting and formative for the way someone sees his or her body. If specific body standards are lauded as acceptable and social status in school or at work depends on meeting those standards, temptation to comply follows.

The physical expectations that come with playing certain sports are another form of social pressure. For instance, those in gymnastics, wrestling, cheerleading, and swimming face pressure to meet specific body types. This pressure may come from parents, coaches, or teammates, and it is frequently internalized. To be the best gymnast or wrestler, one normally faces an expectation for low body weight, or else performance could be impacted. Teenage appearance angst combined with the desire for success and pressure to look like teammates can become overwhelming forces that amplify a negative body image and can potentially lead to an eating disorder. Whether from a parent's extreme standards for weight and physique, jealousy over a sibling's body, the teasing of peers, or adherence to a sport-specific body type, family and friends can create an environment ripe for negative body image.

Media

While the opinions of family and friends weigh heavily on body image, the media also pushes conformity to societal ideals. Television shows, movies, and commercials each play a part in prescribing the "right" body types. Think about the underlying messages that the media communicates regarding who is attractive or unattractive. Often, slender women are portrayed as a love interest, whereas fuller women are cast in less flattering roles. Fit, tall men become heroes while men of smaller stature are less important. Older men are romantic interests of younger women, while older women play grandmother roles. In advertising, the common adage "sex sells" is extremely prevalent, particularly as Americans' cultural standard for how much skin can be revealed steadily increases. Or consider the marketing messages that promise you'll have enhanced desirability if you use certain products. Without them, you are told that you will never achieve that appearance standard.

Examples of the media's impact on body image could go on. While avoiding them all is virtually impossible, it is important to cultivate a recognition of the messaging to guard against their contribution to negative body image. Once you spot the unhelpful influence, instead of accepting it as the truth about you, fill your mind with the truth of who you are in Christ—dearly loved, chosen by God for good works that will last for eternity (Ephesians 1:3–5; 2:8–10). It's a fight to set your mind on things above, but as you do, God will begin to free you from so much negative thinking about your body and appearance (Colossians 3:2).

Social media

As evidenced by the 2023 Surgeon General's report, social media's impact on how we see our bodies has increased dramatically in recent years.[9] The association of social media with harmful effects is so strong that the Surgeon General's report called on legislative action to address it. One scroll through a popular social media platform confronts you with messages of perfect male and female bodies, fashionable clothing for certain body types, unhealthy fitness trends, and seemingly unattainable meal-prepping, workout, or makeup regimens. All serve as incessant reminders of inadequacy. Even social media platforms are aware their content has dramatically increased the experience of bodily dissatisfaction in their users: internal memos from Facebook revealed their awareness that Instagram is toxic for teenage mental health.[10] The sad reality is that these companies seem to care more about the bottom line instead of dealing with the reality that their content fuels negative body image and eating disorders.

Many social media images are altered and not real, but because users cannot always discern the difference, the damage remains. This has given rise to a new phenomenon called "Snapchat dysphoria." This disorder is characterized by an intense, overwhelming need to heavily edit one's appearance on social media. Obsession drives the sufferer to excessively alter images before posting them. Snapchat alone has twenty filters that users can take advantage of to transform anyone's actual appearance to an ideal image. And if twenty filters are not enough, there are apps to purchase that will give the desired look. Experts are alarmed by Snapchat dysphoria not only because it terribly skews body image, but it also leads some sufferers to seek out plastic surgery hoping to alter their face to match a filtered Snapchat picture.[11]

And while social media exposure can threaten anyone's body image, it is especially destructive for children whose brains are not fully developed and are not as equipped to guard against unhelpful external messaging.[12] For this reason, reducing exposure has proved beneficial for overall well-being and mental health, particularly among teenagers and children. In one study participants limited their screen time to thirty minutes a day. According to researchers, this decrease resulted in "significant positive effect and significantly lower levels of anxiety, depression, loneliness, and fear of missing out . . ."[13] These outcomes are especially significant at a time when anxiety, depression, and even suicide rates are on the rise in teens.[14]

The helpful effects of reducing time spent on social media also extend to body image.[15] While lengthy social media use and negative body image are associated, so are less screen time and an improved body image.[16] But the question is, Have we grown so accustomed to perusing social media that we discount the discontent it drives? Has it become such an ingrained habit that we are unwilling to put necessary parameters on it? Wisdom would suggest that we all should take steps to limit time to the recommended thirty minutes a day, unfollow negative influences, or ensure it doesn't interfere with physical needs like sleep and exercise, which also impact mental health. Such steps would benefit both adolescents and adults.[17]

Christians need wisdom from God on how to navigate social media, particularly for adults who seek to protect children from these influences. When exposure to it can generate intense body image issues that enslave sufferers for years, we must ask ourselves if the risks outweigh the benefits, especially as most of its messages are not conducive to a God-honoring body image. Because of this reality, when we work on reframing our appearance expectations—from Scripture not society—it is essential to carefully evaluate our social media usage.

Behavioral contributors

Unsurprisingly, negative body image arises in people with a tendency for low self-esteem, perfectionism, or melancholy temperament.[18] This reality makes personality a definite factor in negative body image as certain traits put one at higher risk for skewed body thoughts. Additionally, certain habits and sin patterns can directly lead to or exacerbate body image issues.

Personality

Individuals with perfectionist tendencies commonly find something about their body offensive, lacking, and flawed. Because they regularly demand high standards of themselves, when those standards go unmet, despair, self-loathing, and destructive thinking result. This response is especially true when it comes to self-imposed physical expectations. An incessant drive for bodily perfection naturally gives way to critical thoughts when bodily preferences go unmet.[19] Combine this perfectionism with negative self-talk, and the result can be an endless cycle of private scolding reinforced by unattainable standards. A perfectionist is prone to be enslaved to negative body image.[20]

For believers who are made perfect through Christ alone, the drive of perfectionism is misguided from the start. The perfectionist seeks control and self-justification, instead of relying on what the Father sent Christ to do in achieving our salvation that is applied by the Spirit. The drive to create a perfect body now can be brought to an end by resting in the hope of eternal perfection that awaits us in Christ.

Temperament and self-esteem

Often those with a melancholy or somber temperament can be more conscious of their own perceived shortcomings. This natural self-consciousness leads them to pay increased attention to areas of physical concern, especially around others. If they regularly view themselves as failing to measure up, low self-esteem will follow. And because the tendency of being self-consciousness about the body can fuel low self-esteem, negative body image usually results. These tendencies may also go on to impact social functioning, which only serves to reinforce self-focus on what is considered "wrong" with their bodies.[21] When a melancholy temperament, low self-esteem, and negative body image are combined, it can cause those who struggle to pull away from meaningful relationships that could help them move past such tendencies.

Physical habits

Physical habits and unconscious patterns also play a role in body dissatisfaction. Habits like pulling at clothing, checking the mirror, or adjusting posture serve as unconscious patterns meant to conceal bothersome flaws and fix appearance. Activities like obsessively monitoring calories or filtering pictures often become mindless efforts to soothe a mind that is preoccupied with negative body image. These habits can temporarily soothe those who are struggling with their body image, but they are also driven by a relentless preoccupation with what others might think about their bodies.[22] When other people are present, those battling body dissatisfaction end up scrupulously monitoring themselves on heightened alert for their approval or disapproval. In the fight against negative body image, growing awareness of these factors, particularly ones that happen subconsciously, is vital.

Sinful tendencies

A few other factors in the behavioral category need to be considered for believers battling negative body image, as various sinful tendencies can also be at play. Fear of man drives body dissatisfaction from the concern that others will make fun of you or not accept you if your body fails to look a certain way. Pride and vanity mark the pursuit of the perfect body that meets the world's standards. Seeking to please people instead of God shows up when efforts for the right body type are driven by the quest for admiration. Selfishness and idolatry become evident when a desire to look a certain way becomes more important than anything else. Coveting, jealousy, and discontent can also characterize negative body image when you want the body that others have rather than being content with how God has made you. Each of these sin struggles can combine in negative body image.

In the end, there may be multiple things we need to focus on when attempting to pursue a God-honoring body image. The way we follow the call to glorify God in the ways we think about our bodies may last a lifetime and shift with age or life circumstances. But the point for believers is that we can engage in the struggle against negative body image through the power of the gospel that changes our hearts, gives us the mind of Christ, equips us with the fruit of the Spirit, and spurs us toward godly living. Through that power, we are not alone in discerning and combating contributors to negative body image.

Physical contributors

Physical features such as congenital birth defects, pregnancy-related changes, and accidents can all contribute to negative body image. These characteristics will need to be addressed with each individual to work through their particular negative body image issues, but because these characteristics impact some people but are not common to all, this section will look at universal factors that disturb body image in most people: genetics, puberty, weight, and aging.

Genetics

Just as you cannot choose the family you are born into, so you have no control over the sex in which you are born or the genes you possess. Many people battle negative body image over things they can never change, barring extreme measures like plastic surgery. It may be facial features like a bump on your nose, an elongated neck, wider-set eyes, or thin lips that trigger negative body image when you look in the mirror. Perhaps a genetic predisposition for premature baldness or short stature serves as constant reminders of physical flaws. Or you might find the shape of your hips, fuller ankles, or extra-long toes particularly bothersome. Your thoughts could be consumed by an inability to be as strong, fast, skinny, or muscular as you want to be. Each of these physical hang-ups undoubtedly contribute to negative body image if we are unable to accept these bodily realities that lie outside our control.

Puberty

The natural developmental stage of adolescence is typified by the experience of puberty in boys ages eleven to fifteen and girls ages nine to fifteen.[23] Bodily changes during puberty can dramatically magnify body image issues, particularly in off-time puberty. Off-time puberty occurs when a teen's experience with the natural transition to physical maturity differs from others their age. In boys, this phenomenon may lead late-maturing individuals to take steroids and supplements to match the muscularity of their more mature peers, or they may begin to disparage their underdeveloped bodies.[24] For young girls whose bodies deposit fat in new areas, body image concerns develop if their understanding of these physical shifts lag behind their changing bodies. The onset of menstruation prior to their peers is often hard enough for girls to handle. But if they perceive their body as "fat" compared to others who have not yet begun puberty, their bodily distress exacerbates. In addition to their own observations and distress, the physical differences experienced by girls at younger age and boys at a later age often results in ridicule from their peers, which makes matters worse. However, if pre-teens and teens rightly understand these changes as part of God's good plans in the maturity process, they will be equipped to accept them more readily.

Weight

Weight can be a definite contributor that most if not all people will deal with at some point in life. Maybe you've faced teasing for being underweight, or perhaps, being overweight has brought ridicule and hurtful comments. Even feeling just a few pounds too heavy can impact body image. Someone who feels they are underweight may become obsessed with changing their body to add muscle and match those who are bigger and stronger. When this drive begins to consume, it can turn into muscle dysphoria. Likewise, a person who perceives themselves to be overweight may stop eating meals to drastically reach the weight they want, but soon those skipped meals begin to fuel an eating disorder. Then, the person who just wants to lose five pounds may grow so dependent on exercise that it becomes excessive, causes physical harm, and again, lays the foundation for an eating disorder.

Weight can be a challenge for a season or sometimes for a lifetime. If weight gain or loss efforts are driven by negative body image, they can cross the line from seeking to glorify God in how you treat your body to striving to glorify self by the way your body looks. The goal for Christians is to pursue reasonable, healthy eating and exercise habits with the aim of wisely stewarding the body God has given them.

Aging

The aging process alters physical appearance, though it is a commonly overlooked contributor to bodily dissatisfaction. While everyone ages, some people accept and endure the resulting physical changes better than others. For women, dissatisfaction can arise due to new wrinkles, graying hair, and age spots. Additionally, the bodily shifts that menopause brings may be more troubling than any other physical changes experienced at other points in life. With certain hormonal fluctuations come natural shifts in fat storage around the midsection, instead of the hips—which is where it was prior to menopause. While men may not be as troubled by the superficial effects of aging like new gray hairs and wrinkles, what they can find most disconcerting are the new aches and pains that limit their physical mobility. Worsening eyesight or hearing may create physical disabilities for the first time. For men, if these changes are overwhelming, they might find themselves plunged beyond negative body image into despair and shame.

Without a healthy ability to alter bodily expectations to match this new stage of life, negative body image is inevitable. While oftentimes worsening for women, aging men may experience significant body image issues for the first time. Whether it's accelerated hair loss, weight gain, sagging skin, slowing gait, increased joint pain, advance of chronic disease, or the need for dentures, age-related challenges are inescapable. And so are the temptations to view the body harshly.

To understand the weight of these challenges, ponder the following personal, frank admission from Luke Timothy Johnson in his book, *The Revelatory Body*, where he refers to aging as the "gentlest signature of mortality."[25] Detailing his "bodily experience of diminishment," Johnson is quite candid about his personal struggles:

> The decade of my sixties, especially the last half, was the most revealing in terms of physical change. All at once, it seems, the warranty elapses, and everything starts to fall apart. It

> is, of course, not "all at once," but just another stage in a long process. But now I am alert to my weaknesses more than I am to my strengths. . . . My body now seems to me less a reliable friend than an unpredictable and sometimes resentful companion. My eyes are worse, my hearing is bad . . . and arthritis stabs me with pain . . . I have hypertension. My weight insists on staying. My hair is white and thinning. . . . My lower back is in very bad shape. I now need to walk an hour every day, and faithfully do back exercises, simply to remain mobile. I don't even think about picking up the ball and throwing it; the thought of the consequent pain in my shoulder is sufficient to prevent any such fantasy. Indeed I cannot really remember my muscular and athletic body. . . . [M]y aging process is absolutely normal. But I still don't like it.[26]

Despite physical decline, Johnson admits that "the emotional entailments of aging are perhaps the most complex and difficult to disentangle."[27] These emotional aspects are precisely why body image must be recognized as an important part of Christian faithfulness even in old age. With physical decline come thoughts and emotions about those waning abilities.[28]

While some assume body image is not a struggle pertinent to them, the impact of aging will eventually provide us all an opportunity for troublesome experiences of our bodies. Christians should be on guard against the natural, physical contributors to negative body image if we are serious about glorifying God in their bodies. And as the aging process can drum up many new body issues in men, another component in male body image needs highlighting.

MALES AND NEGATIVE BODY IMAGE

While 70 percent of girls want to be thinner, thinking that a smaller appearance would improve their lives, boys are not as forthcoming about their appearance desires.[29] That is why negative body image in boys is tougher to tackle. The experience of distorted body thoughts in boys has long been overlooked because until twenty years ago, male body image surveys used questions similar to the ones asked of girls. Because body image in boys was measured according to the thinness standard for girls, struggles over appearance and body type were missed for years.[30] This oversight perpetuated the notion that boys do not struggle with their physical form and appearance ideals. Thus, body image has been commonly labeled a female issue. But misunderstanding body image issues in boys can cause many to silently struggle with body dissatisfaction.

While negative body image in adult males tends to focus on baldness and unwanted weight gain, the biggest source for body dissatisfaction in adolescent boys lies in a desire to be more muscular, taller, or stronger. In more extreme cases, the individual experiences reverse anorexia, where he is fearful of his perceived small stature and perceived weaknesses, leading to extreme corrective measures. More recently, reverse anorexia was termed muscle dysmorphia or bigorexia and falls within the classification of body dysphoric disorder.[31]

Additionally, in a time of rampant childhood obesity, a different group of boys undergo harmful practices such as purging and taking laxatives to lose weight, like girls with distorted body image.

But whether it is weight, face shape, stature, birth defect, perceived attractiveness, or another subjectively labeled flaw, dissatisfaction with the body is not the perspective that Scripture teaches. But before we can move toward a biblical view of the body, it is necessary to first identify our struggles with negative body image. If you answer yes to two or more of these questions, it would be wise to seek help for negative body image. If you are mentoring or counseling someone who seems to struggle with body image issues, you can use these questions to help you learn more about their particular body image struggles.

REFLECTION QUESTIONS

Assessing Your Current Body Image

Answer all the questions below that apply to you now.

1. Do thoughts about your body distract you from daily tasks?

2. When you use social media, does it encourage negative thoughts about your body?

3. Are you strongly concerned about physical changes that have occurred in your body due to puberty, aging, or maternity?

4. Do you regularly try to hide the flaws you perceive in your body?

Chapter 3

DISORDERED RESPONSES TO NEGATIVE BODY IMAGE

Nora is thirteen years old and spends lots of time looking in the mirror. What she sees there is not what others see. She sees someone who is fat and needs to be thinner. Even though the physical changes that trouble her are from puberty, she hates the way her body looks. So she plans ways to lose weight. First, she'll start with what she eats. She'll never eat sugar again. Then, she'll run a mile every day and add 100 crunches every other day. Surely, this plan will help her lose weight. If not, she can always do more.

You might know someone like Nora whose negative body image is leading them to negative behaviors. Sadly, negative body image often leads to disordered responses. When we pass that mental body picture through a subjective filter and judge our appearance as lacking, behaviors aimed at fixing our "flaws" usually follow. To be clear, negative body image alone will not necessarily cause disordered responses or an eating disorder; other triggers are usually involved, like going through a traumatic event, having a desire for control, experiencing ridicule, lacking emotional regulation, or being driven by perfectionism. However, disorders are fueled by distorted thinking about the body, so when we address negative body image, we should also be alert to the possibility of an eating disorder or other problematic reactions as well. And while not as concerning as the diagnosable disorders covered in this chapter, Christians should guard against milder responses to negative body image. Some of these reactions include yo-yo dieting, spending excessive amounts of money on the latest supplement or equipment promising quick results, wasting hours each day on social media following fitness gurus, scheduling unnecessary plastic surgeries to fix superficial flaws, or developing such a preoccupation with meal and exercise planning that it interrupts your daily routine.

WHAT IS AN EATING DISORDER?

Eating disorders are on the rise with the three most prevalent being anorexia, bulimia, and binge-eating disorder.[1] While there are several other types of eating or feeding disorders, this chapter will focus on the most common that are typically associated with negative body image, beginning with anorexia and bulimia. The fifth edition of the *Diagnostic and Statistical Manual of Mental Disorders (DSM-5)* lists three qualifiers for an anorexia or bulimia diagnosis. First, there must be an intentional effort to restrict calories that results in weight too low for normal health. Second, there must be an intense fear of weight gain to the extent that it controls thoughts and actions. Third, overwhelming disapproval of the body as a whole or a specific part accompanies the eating disorder.[2]

Though eating disorders primarily occur in females ages twelve to thirty-five, anyone can be diagnosed, and many factors influence their development.[3] If friends or family battled an eating disorder, that reality can play a significant role. When academic pressures increase or when sports expectations grow, particularly in sports like gymnastics, ballet, swimming, wrestling, and cycling, eating disorders often arise.[4] They are regularly associated with certain behavioral tendencies like perfectionism, especially as perfectionists excel at the discipline that eating disorders require.[5] Predictably, exposure to television, movies, and social media can heighten the risks too. As influencers gain fame for fitness and eating regimens, their search for more followers can press them into a disorder, which, in turn, influences their fans. When those things are glorified, disordered thinking, eating, and exercising follow.

Clearly, numerous factors contribute to eating disorder development, in addition to negative body image. While more disorders exist than can be addressed here, those most linked to severe body displeasure require definite attention and help.

TYPES OF DISORDERED RESPONSES TO NEGATIVE BODY IMAGE

Because many people with a negative body image go on to attempt to change their bodies to match their ideal form, unhealthy measures take many forms. These measures may mean restricting food or self-imposed starvation, as in anorexia, which has the highest mortality rate of all mental health issues.[6] Similarly, bulimia nervosa can develop, which also has the goal of weight loss but is pursued through self-induced vomiting rather than starvation. Binge-eating disorder is akin to bulimia in its excessive consumption of food in a single-sitting, but unlike bulimia it does not compensate for the binge. Though eating disorders predominantly occur in females ages 12–35, one-third of those who suffer are males.[7] And, while it may come at a surprise, a small percent of women age sixty and up also experience them.[8]

Anorexia nervosa

Anorexia nervosa is characterized by extreme bias against the body that is evident in beliefs, thoughts, feelings, and actions. Irrational beliefs about physical appearance give way to destructive thoughts that mix with despair and lead to self-inflicted harm. The anorexic holds an inaccurate perception of her body and is driven by a skewed ideal that requires extreme vigilance to achieve.[9] Attaching her self-worth to these vigilant activities, she measures success by her ability to deprive herself of food, burn sufficient calories with exercise, avoid social eating situations, and more. Her value is found in the number on the scale, and any negativity that arises from "failure" to achieve her goals only perpetuates the distorted body image.

To try to calm her mind, an anorexic incessantly monitors her body with constant weighing, checking the mirror, and touching undesirable areas. She not only avoids social situations, but also any clothing that fails to conceal her body the way she desires, preferring to wear mostly baggy, loose-fitting clothing. These checking and avoidance behavior patterns are part of the cyclical nature of negative body image and appearance obsession, but such activities never fix the issue. Her misperceptions only continue.

Each thought, emotion, and action that plagues the sufferer revolves around the goal of having a desirable body. This incessant process makes reversing these habits challenging, especially when there is denial of the dangers that low weight presents. Even when confronted with potential medical issues, the anorexic often rejects the seriousness of her condition.[10] Health problems resulting from long-term self-starvation pose a variety of alarming threats to physical well-being.

Anorexics face many physical problems, and no part of the body is spared. In the most extreme cases, 5 percent of sufferers die.[11] In less severe cases, the long-term effects of malnutrition are still serious. Externally, anorexics look malnourished, underweight, bony, pale, or sick. Their skin dries out, becoming bruised, yellow, and covered with fine hair growth. They experience greater cold sensitivity due to a decrease in body fat as well as an inability to regulate their body temperature. The hair on their head falls out, and nails grow brittle.[12]

Internally, more physiological consequences emerge. Muscles and bones weaken, even to the point of breaking. Osteoporosis may develop, which comes from a decrease in bone mass density, a condition nearly impossible to reverse and one that only worsens in time. Those with anorexia experience trouble thinking, mood swings, and memory issues. The eating disorder also wreaks havoc hormonally. Growth is stunted. Menstruation stops. Females struggle to get pregnant. The risks of miscarriage and postpartum depression also increase. Kidney stones and kidney failure can happen. Important mineral levels like potassium, magnesium, and sodium decrease. Digestive issues like constipation and bloating arise. Ultimately, the severe and continual lack of food affects the heart. Low blood pressure results, causing fainting and dizziness. A decreased heart rate follows, then heart palpitations, and eventually heart failure. Anorexia nervosa destroys multiple body systems—gastrointestinal, endocrine, respiratory, circulatory, musculoskeletal, neurological, and integumentary.[13] God simply did not create his embodied image-bearers with the ability to endure the effects of long-term starvation.

Bulimia nervosa disorder

Bulimia nervosa sufferers experience the same distortions in body image, but their coping methods differ from the willful starvation in anorexia. While bulimia does not cause the same degree of malnourishment, sufferers still engage in behaviors that harm the body.[14] Bulimics cycle between excessive bouts of eating followed by compensating behaviors to purge by self-induced vomiting or laxative use.[15] On average, a binging and purging episode occurs twice a week, but diagnosis only requires one episode a week for three consecutive months.[16] Sometimes, binges are triggered after eating foods considered off limits or by consuming too many calories for the day. Then, to compensate or punish oneself for these dietary failures, the bulimic will purge to counteract the excess calories.[17] Like anorexia, bulimia is characterized by negative body image and disdain for one's physical appearance. As with anorexia diagnoses, females dominate bulimia diagnoses, comprising about 90 percent of cases.[18] Because sufferers feel ashamed over their binging and purging events, most hide their struggles, even from loved ones.

While bulimics do not experience the same extreme weight loss and its effects as anorexics, significant health issues still arise from the regular efforts to purge. Stomach acid from frequent vomiting can advance tooth decay and cause other oral problems. In severe cases, the esophagus ruptures. Callouses develop on the fingers used to purge. When laxatives are combined with vomiting, low fluid and electrolyte levels cause serious medical complications. Dehydration occurs, which also comes with serious problems that affect the entire body and can be life-threatening. And repeated laxative use can cause rectal prolapse in some cases, with regular constipation issues continuing in mild cases even when purging ends.[19]

Binge-eating disorder

Binge-eating disorder includes the extreme food binges that bulimics engage in, but it does not include an offsetting purge. Occasions of binge-eating typically follow a trigger. It could be an unexpected phone call, a stressful meeting, relationship strife, poor job review, or other tense, nerve-racking events. To control the resulting emotions and in efforts to calm down, the binge-eater secretly consumes large amounts of food. Often, sufferers report an inability to stop the overeating episode, which is then followed by feelings of shame and self-loathing.[20] And, as with anorexia and bulimia, mental health issues coincide, particularly depression and anxiety.

While not always a direct equivalent, the physical ramifications from frequent bouts of excessive eating are predominantly associated with being overweight and obese, as regularly overeating leads to weight gain and the chronic diseases that typically follow.[21] While these realities are difficult to come to grips with, the ramifications of binge-eating disorder can be serious. Diseases such as type 2 diabetes, high blood pressure, high cholesterol, heart attack, stroke, certain cancers, fatty liver, osteoarthritis, coronary artery disease, and gallstones result from carrying excess weight for too long. Sufferers need help addressing their behaviors with food and exercise as the physical consequences of binge-eating disorder may end up being life-threatening.[22]

Disordered eating

While signs of eating disorders are more evident, actions associated with disordered eating are more covert. Disordered eating, though not a diagnosable eating disorder, involves similar behaviors that, if not kept in check or curbed, will likely intensify into a diagnosis. Regularly skipping meals classifies as disordered eating, especially if missing a meal becomes a marker of success or achievement. Even fasting can become problematic if done from an obsessive mindset. If dieting and cutting calories develop into compulsive behaviors, a full-blown eating disorder may not be far away. Avoidance of entire food groups, a growing list of "off-limits" food, a rigidity against splurging, or conversely, times of hoarding and over-consuming food are all warning signs of disordered eating. Taking pills designed to induce weight loss or cause unnatural muscle growth, beginning to purge by vomiting or taking laxatives are all problematic behaviors that promote eating disorders. When emotional regulation is combined with disordered eating actions, the stage is set for a diagnosable condition. If a negative body image also plays a role in perpetuating these behaviors, all the elements of an eating disorder are in place.[23]

Bigorexia nervosa

Unlike other disorders, bigorexia or muscle dysphoria primarily afflicts males who hold an unrealistic view of how muscular their bodies should look. Like other body image-related issues, severe bodily dissatisfaction fuels bigorexia, as these individuals are never content with their musculature. While not all experts consider it an eating disorder, many link it to body dysmorphic disorder. And as it is often fueled by social media, rates have drastically risen in recent years, which is of additional concern as negative body image and eating disorders remain understudied in males.[24] For these reasons, some males may be completely unaware of their struggle with bigorexia.

Social media is largely to blame for the increase in this condition. Young adult males and those into bodybuilding are the most affected, and the condition is evidenced by a preoccupation with weight training, steroid use, calorie-counting, and obsession with their image on social media. Regularly posting photos in the gym or following fitness influencers who promote similar behaviors and extreme exercise may be signs. Emotional outbursts are common, whether from an influx of testosterone or to pump themselves up during a lifting session. Their social lives revolve around the gym. Extra time and money get spent on planning and maintaining strict eating routines and even pursuing calf, bicep, or pec implants. Any remaining mental space is devoted to scheduling the next lift, finding other exercises to add bulk, and researching new supplements that might help them reach the next level in the gym.

As appearance concerns perpetuate this body dysphoria, these sufferers' lives revolve around building muscle mass. In extreme cases, bigorexics refuse to leave their house, shackled by their perception of an insufficient body. They fixate for hours on their appearance, refusing to entertain the possibility that their obsession is unhealthy and erroneous. Combine these severe distortions with the ceaseless pressure from social media to have a specific body type, and these males will commit to whatever measures are necessary to be big and muscular.[25]

Gender dysphoria

While gender dysphoria is not an eating disorder, it must be understood in the context of negative body image, and more appropriately, body dysmorphic disorder, as it describes a severe, consuming dissatisfaction with being male or female. Whether the distress centers on a specific body part or the body in general, the issue of dysphoria and skewed body image remains. Two types of gender dysphoria exist. Early onset most often begins in young children and decreases with age.[26] Rapid onset appears later around puberty, as do many other body image issues.[27] The increasing rates of gender dysphoria suggest many cases of it should be considered a social contagion, one spreading among friends and through social media, particularly among teenage girls.[28]

Given this increase, gender dysphoria is an area Christians, especially counselors, should be ready and able to discuss. For this reason, a few applications of a biblical worldview will be considered, as this can certainly be a difficult topic to discuss. Even more, simply being open to listen to struggles of gender dysphoria can go a long way in gaining a person's trust. Willingness to step in and help sort through the difficulties will often lead to a reciprocated willingness to hear wisdom and input from others, as the internal battles and consuming struggles that arise often make sufferers feel desperate. With such confusing and alarming messages coming from the culture, Christians must be able to share the hope of the gospel and comforting truths of our sovereign Creator who purposefully designs his embodied image-bearers in soul and body. In this way, Christians can lovingly offer the unique help and clarity that only comes from a biblical worldview.

To be clear, gender dysphoria should be distinguished from transgenderism. Someone struggling with gender dysphoria is different from someone who gives into those feelings and choses to identify as the opposite sex. A believer may genuinely struggle with gender dysphoria but cannot condone transgenderism (Genesis 1:26–27). Because of this, Christians must not advocate gender-affirming surgeries, treatments, or medications.

Compassion for those who struggle with gender discomfort is essential, yet a biblical body image affirms the blessing of being born either male or female and accepting the sovereignly planned, detailed ways that God designed us. Christians should reject the idea that one can change their sex or even the separation of gender from biological sex. The American Psychiatric Association defines gender dysphoria as the dissatisfaction that arises if a person's gender identity differs from the gender assigned at birth. According to this line of thinking, gender dysphoria is a disconcerting feeling of being born in the wrong body. Though experts support treatment, that treatment often advocates for eliminating the bodily dissatisfaction by changing the body rather than addressing the distortions in one's sense of self.[29] One issue with this approach is its promotion that the problem is not with the mind but with the body. So gender-affirming care is often the next step. To mitigate the dysphoria, hormones may be given to slow or stop the natural effects of puberty along with procedures to cut off or alter healthy body parts.

A gender dysphoria diagnosis relies on redefining realities, including a false separation of biological sex and gender. Instead of biological, physical realities confirming one's personhood, one's feelings are taken as the basis of identity. In other words, visible body parts are cast aside if they conflict with a mental perception. This approach presses for a disembodied living, one that suggests the way to soothe the mind is by ignoring or even altering the body. But God designed us as embodied beings with a psychosomatic connection between mind and body, a connection meant to promote flourishing. The trouble with disconnecting mental from physical health to function as a whole person will ultimately be unsuccessful because it goes against God's embodied, psychosomatic design.

Furthermore, it's important to recognize that encouraging someone with gender dysphoria to get medicine and surgery is not the way all other negative body image issues are treated. Experts don't support the distorted thinking of an anorexic by encouraging liposuction. Bigorexics are not counseled to get implants to add the mass they believe they lack. Bulimics who purge multiple times a week to control weight are not told that their efforts are succeeding. Compassionate care means helping all who struggle with negative body image to see themselves the way God sees them.

Taking a close look at these disorders shows us that negative body image seldom stays contained in the mind. It often drives the sufferer to take actions that are meant to relieve body dissatisfaction. While these reactions may start small, if not kept in check and fought against, they can lead to disordered responses, or even a diagnosable condition.

REFLECTION QUESTIONS

1. Could your current view of your body lead to an eating disorder?

2. Do you have any disordered eating tendencies? If so, what are some steps you could take to address this issue?

3. Would friends and family say you spend too much time working out and are overly concerned with building muscle mass?

Chapter 4

THE WORLD'S RESPONSES TO NEGATIVE BODY IMAGE

Jackie, who just had a new baby, is struggling with her body image more than ever. Every glance in the mirror is a reminder of excess weight she's failed to get off. Each time she opens social media to post a picture of her newborn serves to reinforce her body dissatisfaction, especially seeing other moms. Their perfect-looking bodies and seemingly perfect kids make Jackie feel like she needs something else, something that will help her change how she sees her body.

Jackie, like so many others, tried to deal with her negative body image in a variety of ways: positive self-talk, body resilience, self-improvement strategies, bettering her relationship with her body, and loving her body. These are just a few of the solutions offered by our world. The trouble is that many of these responses to negative body image locate the solution within the individual, which is contrary to a biblical worldview. We can never be enough within ourselves to tackle our problems, which is why we need Christ. In this chapter, we will briefly consider plastic surgery, the body positivity movement, and popular therapeutic approaches to negative body image like cognitive-behavioral therapy and the sociocultural model. As we walk through these attempts to deal with the problem of negative body image, we will note how, because of God's common grace, many of these secular approaches unknowingly rely on biblical principles in certain aspects of how they respond to body dissatisfaction. It is important to discern the strengths of these approaches while also avoiding their weaknesses.

THE BEAUTY INDUSTRY

According to our image-obsessed culture, if you are dissatisfied with an aspect of your body, there's nothing wrong with trying to fix it: liposuction, nose jobs, hair transplants, and tummy tucks. And don't forget all the lifts and implants: forehead, butt, face, thigh, eyelid, arm, neck, breast, lip, calf, pec, cheek, and bicep. The list could go on. Bottom line, if we are concerned about a part of our body, we can find a doctor who will alter it. There are many times when plastic surgery is needed, for example fixing a congenital birth defect, disfigurement following an accident, breast reconstruction after cancer, and others. But turning to a cosmetic procedure to alleviate negative body image requires wise counsel and discussion.

The number of plastic surgeries has greatly increased in recent years.[1] With this rise, it should come as no surprise that the complications people experience have also increased.[2] Risks are involved with any surgery. But with more people seeking to alter their bodies, more patients are suffering extreme disfigurement, nerve damage, life-threatening infections, blood clots, even death. Despite the potential harm, a 50 percent increase in surgeries came following COVID when people regularly saw themselves on virtual meetings and were stuck indoors spending extra time on social media.[3] Surgeries that aim to slow or reverse age progression have also grown in popularity, especially among those thirty and under. This desire to fix perceived flaws influenced by social media has driven experts to coin terms such as "Selfie-awareness, Snapchat dysmorphia, Instagram face, ZOOM boom effect, and TikTok Face."[4] The increase in procedures has been so dramatic that plastic surgeons themselves are taking to social media to discourage unnecessary cosmetic surgery in younger populations.[5]

There are legitimate reasons for plastic surgery, and some cosmetic procedures may be medically necessary, minimally invasive, and less expensive. But if surgeries are costly or become too important to us, examining our motives is a good first step. Don't we have to do that with all of our decisions? Some questions to ask ourselves might be: Am I depending on a procedure to help me accept my body? Am I tempted to believe the only way to improve my emotional or mental health is to surgically alter my body? Would I be taking on undue risks to my physical health or require lengthy recovery time that takes me away from God-given responsibilities?

Seeking ultimate contentment and satisfaction in anything besides the Lord will fail to satisfy us—we are made to worship God and find joy, meaning, and purpose in him. So we must take care to examine our reasons for wanting plastic surgery. Following after our culture's recommendations for what is beautiful and acceptable will always leave us feeling inadequate. Seeking to "fix" our bodies with plastic surgeries will never provide the lasting peace found only in the God of peace who wants our hearts to find freedom and rest when contented in him alone.

BODY POSITIVITY MOVEMENT

A quick search on Instagram for body positivity will result in well over twelve million posts supporting the value of all people's bodies, no matter their physical makeup or measurements. The movement promotes loving yourself no matter your shape or size and has pushed back against societal beauty norms. On the surface, it looks like an appealing way to combat negative body image.

Christians would agree with the body positivity movement that all people deserve to be treated with respect. No one should be discriminated against because of their physical appearance. While the body positivity movement does not ground their views in Scripture, it is biblical to advocate for the respectful, equal treatment of others. As Christians we should advocate for the exact same things, except that we prioritize God's Word as our foundation and guide for showing us how to treat others.

Although Christians agree that all people should be treated with dignity, we need wisdom when considering this movement as a viable remedy for negative body image. Christians should be wary to look beyond the surface claims of body positivity movement. The movement can harm its supporters by minimizing the importance of their physical health. Sadly proponents condemn weight loss efforts, discrediting research that links obesity and chronic disease.[6] Their resistance to pursuing a healthier body weight is so strong that "fat activists vehemently discourage weight loss and any effort to increase wellness. They not only demand representation but want to silence all forms of dissent."[7]

Though the body positivity movement calls for loving yourself no matter your size or shape, the underlying implication is that your body—your physical health—is not important. But as Christians who steward their bodies as representatives of Christ, our physical well-being is important—it matters to God. Elevating mental health while ignoring physical health is to deny our embodied connection, which will never achieve lasting results. For these reasons, believers should pause before embracing the body positivity movement as way viable way to handle harmful body thoughts. Once aware of its core beliefs, Christians would be wise to move away from this secular worldview to a biblical one that can more holistically and helpfully address negative body image.

TWO THERAPEUTIC MODELS

In psychology, the two most popular approaches to negative body image are the cognitive-behavioral and sociocultural models. Interestingly, both have elements that agree with Scripture by showing that body image can be positively impacted by reforming thoughts, actions, and influences. While Christians ought not elevate these models above Scripture, we can highlight where they depend on biblical truths.

The cognitive-behavioral model seeks to change thoughts and actions to move someone beyond a particular struggle. The model distinguishes between historical and proximal factors that shape body image over time. Historical factors arise based on previous life situations that create beliefs and patterns of thought about the body. These beliefs and patterns then weigh on feelings and actions. Proximal factors stem from current life events that further develop body image and can also be influenced by long-established historical ones. When a current situation like stepping on a scale triggers previously formed beliefs and patterns of thought and emotions, actions related to negative body image result.[8] This model attempts to alter the underlying thinking that influences these behaviors.

The sociocultural model considers how influences like family, friends, and media contribute to unrealistic body standards. For those suffering from negative body image, this approach examines how relationships perpetuate cultural body standards that communicate the way bodies "should" look. As the standards become internalized, bodily satisfaction or dissatisfaction results, depending upon how much that person's appearance matches the perceived societal ideal. This model is especially concerned with identifying subtle messages that these influences generate and then working to limit or avoid altogether their effect on negative body image formation.[9]

Both approaches contain biblical truths. The cognitive-behavioral model labels and modifies destructive thoughts that lead to harmful feelings and actions, which is also a goal of Scripture. As the Holy Spirit illumines God's truth, believers identify wrong thoughts and emotions. Then, in obedience to God's Word, we strive to apply it to our lives and address sinful behaviors. The sociocultural model assesses cultural standards conveyed through relationships. Then, the model considers how these messages are internalized to understand what is acceptable. In similar ways, believers derive their understanding of self-worth from Scripture, not society. Strengthened by relationships with like-minded believers and informed by God's Word, Christians form their body image. Understanding how these secular models address body image help us compare them to a biblical approach toward a God-glorifying body image.[10] And while each method may reflect biblical truths, they ultimately fall short in altering negative body image, as they are devoid of the divine power to change found only in the gospel of Christ and empowered by the Spirit. Only through the indwelling Holy Spirit can believers gain progressive victory over distorted and sinful thinking, even that which characterizes negative body image.

REFLECTION QUESTIONS

1. Have you pursued worldly remedies for a negative body image before?

2. If so, did it fall short of changing how you thought about your body? Why will the world's ways never provide the answer we need for negative body image or any struggle for that matter?

Chapter 5

GOD'S WORD AND NEGATIVE BODY IMAGE

Thomas used to work on his farm from dawn to dusk. He was constantly active—tending to the crops, land, and all the animals. The only time he stopped was to sit down at a meal with his family and to get a good night's rest. But now, his body is failing him. He can barely get around his house, let alone care for the farm like he once did. Every movement serves as a constant reminder of what his body can no longer do. He spends hours in his chair, bemoaning his current physical state and hating his body for how it limits him now. Thomas's wife worries that he might be battling depression in this new, unwanted season.

As believers, we look primarily to Scripture for guidance in all areas of life, and it is no different with body image. Because we all have a body image, and frequently have a negative one, as Christians we need to spend time developing a biblical perspective in this area. Gaining a biblical perspective requires that we first identify any wrong views that we hold about the body. After we've identified and rejected any lies or half-truths we've accepted, we can then embrace God's view of the body. With it, we will be equipped to combat negative body image struggles, relinquish our own flawed and insufficient frameworks, and see our body as God does. And because the body matters to him, it is important to remember that how we think, feel, and act reflects what we believe about our bodies. Striving to glorify God even in the body means continually reflecting on what he says about it.

LIES CHRISTIANS BELIEVE ABOUT THE BODY

Having a biblical view of the body may first require you to address an errant one, and I don't necessarily mean a negative body image. Christians tend to devalue the body. There are biblical examples of this, as we will see in the Corinthian church, and I have also personally experienced this in my struggle with anorexia and over-exercise. During that time, I neglected proper care for my body and was not motivated to glorify God in my body, let alone think biblically about it. Additionally, during my time in ministry and seminary I noticed a similar mindset of neglect toward the body among believers. While working in the local church, I dealt with the physical effects of long-term stress as I failed to rightly care for my well-being. I also saw coworkers battle heart palpitations, high blood pressure, anxiety attacks, insomnia, ulcers, and other stress-related health consequences. I also witnessed many seminarians' health visibly deteriorate while completing their seminary degrees.

This brings us to the final indicator that Christians may fail to rightly think about their bodies. And while it is a difficult topic, the difficultly doesn't mean we can overlook it. When comparing the most religious states and most obese states, there is definite overlap.[1] This does not mean being a Christian makes you fat or that cultural factors aren't at play. But a biblical conception of the body should motivate a basic level of care for physical health. However, the body is easy to neglect when you have a low view of it. That's why, given this overlap of the most religious and most obese states, it is at least worth asking how our faith impacts the care we care for our bodies.

If an apathetic or dismissive view of the body persists, it will hamper our ability to accurately see it through the lens of Scripture, which will contribute to negative body image. Such a view needs reevaluating before we can continue. Assess your own posture toward the body as we consider the followings reasons Christians may hold a low view of it. Although these views of the body are all too common in Christian circles, you might be surprised that they aren't necessarily biblical.

1. *We apply the image of God to the soul and not the body.* Scripture never locates the image of God exclusively in the soul. God created us as embodied beings who are unified yet distinct, immaterial and material, soul and body, men and women. It is this embodied existence that he declares very good. And only as his embodied image-bearers can we keep his commands and experience a relationship with our Creator while enjoying his creation (Genesis 1:26–31).

2. *We view holiness as a spiritual pursuit that is hindered by physical matters.* Believing that holiness is purely a spiritual pursuit and that the body is inherently sinful misunderstands sin's total corruption of embodied humanity. The fall brought consequences of spiritual and physical death from which we need complete restoration in Christ (Genesis 2:17). Because sin affects both body and spirit, Christians pursue an embodied holiness, one where our whole self is sanctified (2 Corinthians 7:1; 1 Thessalonians 5:23).

3. *We miss the full promise of glorification.* If we lack awareness of what future glorification means for the body, we will likely devalue it in the present. Instead, we must remember that when we hope for the new heavens and new earth, we are yearning for a day when we will be gloriously resurrected, re-embodied men and women living in a re-created, perfect physical world (Philippians 3:20–21; Revelation 21).

4. *We forget that just as Christ took on a body in the incarnation, he remains embodied.* This wrong thinking can cause us to overlook the significance of Christ's physical existence for our own and forget that he will transform our perishable bodies to be like his imperishable body (Philippians 3:20–21).

5. *We are confused about the meaning of* "sarx," *the Greek word for flesh.* Paul often uses *sarx*, or "the flesh," to describe sin nature and our natural inclination to disobey God. But this is not its only usage. *Sarx* also holds a neutral meaning for the physical flesh of the body, in addition to the flesh of sinful nature. Without distinguishing between these uses and always linking sinful

flesh to our physical body, we might read Scripture and view the body as the sole source of evil.

6. *We misconstrue Paul's statement that physical training is only of some value.* While godliness is certainly valuable in every way, Christians ought not neglect the body. In context, Paul's comment about physical training is not saying that it is unnecessary. He makes the statement when writing to Timothy about the danger of those who place excessive restrictions on physical matters, specifically marriage and the enjoyment of certain foods (1 Timothy 4:1–8). So his instruction to pursue godliness is a pursuit that remains connected to physical matters. Furthermore, because our bodies impact our ability to minister, bodily training is of definite value when it fuels a life of godliness. Paul's statement about physical training is not meant to diminish the benefits of physical training, but rather to emphasize the importance of training in godliness.

7. *We make conclusions about the body based on individual verses read apart from context.* In Romans 7:24, Paul laments his battle against his sin nature and seeks rescue from his body that is subject to death. Still, we cannot sum up an entire view of the body from Paul's experience as described in Romans 7. In chapter 6, he commands believers to use their bodies as instruments of righteousness (6:13), and in chapter 8, he writes that our adoption will be complete when our bodies are redeemed (8:23). If the body can be used in righteousness and its redemption completes our adoption as God's children, then we cannot use one verse to disregard it.

8. *We assume the body's insignificance based on its temporary separation from the soul.* Upon salvation, we

experience instant justification but not instant glorification (Romans 10:10). While we have been raised to life from spiritual death, we still await physical death. Logically, we must die physically, we cannot die spiritually, since this is the fate from which Christ saved us. Though we will be temporarily disembodied in death, our soul with the Lord and our body in decay, both will be fully restored (2 Corinthians 5:1–9). The sequence of restoration is logical and does not imply the body's insignificance. Rather, the body is significant because it is restored (Romans 8:11).

To see our bodies as God does, it is critical to guard against these viewpoints as each one devalues the body. Such an outlook toward the body will only support negative body image. Having unpacked these misconceptions about the body, we need a fresh, biblical perspective. Body image should focus on what Scripture affirms about the body. Agreeing with God's description of the body is a powerful antidote to negative body image.

A BIBLICAL FRAMEWORK BRINGS PEACE

This section considers several verses that provide the pieces for a biblical framework through which we can pass the mental picture of our body. A negative body image occurs from filtering our body's mental picture through self-defined or culturally-defined ideals to deem it acceptable or unacceptable. But when we switch out the framework that filters our body image, a better judgment can be made. The result is a life that can be poured out for God instead of lived in service to ourselves, and we can have the peace that comes from not having to live up to some unattainable ideal.

Instead of seeing through societal standards and skewed expectations, Christians look through God's Word and accept his conclusions about our physical form. By filtering our body image through the framework of Scripture, we choose to let God define our worth. In this way, we will see our bodies as God sees them.

We have already looked at how Scripture grounds us in truth about our bodies, but how do we live those truths out in our world? One of the most helpful passages is 1 Corinthians 6:12–20, as it helps us define biblical principles that Christians can use to form a God-honoring body image.

1 Corinthians 6:12–20

First Corinthians 6:12–20 serves as a primary text to learn a biblical view of the body, and understanding it can offer tremendous support when confronting negative body image. The Corinthian believers had lots of issues that Paul wrote to correct, from sexual sin to the Lord's Supper to marriage questions, to name just a few. Interestingly, the body was a topic that Paul brought up several times, using it in a variety of ways to communicate a few different themes. For example, he wrote of the body as the temple of the Holy Spirit (6:19), the body's involvement in sanctification (9:24–27), and the significance of Christ's body in the Lord Supper (11:23–29). He compared the need for Christians to use their gifts in the church just as the body needs all its parts (12:12–27), and went into detail about resurrected bodies (15:35–58). So why all this talk on the body to the Corinthians?

Paul wrote to a group of Christians who were influenced by a belief system that concluded the body did not matter: Gnosticism. Spawning Christological heresies, this belief system influenced Christian thought on resurrection. Gnostics taught God was so much greater than the physical world that he could have nothing to do with it. They focused on pursuing a higher, spiritual knowledge, which led them to disregard physical things, like the body. As a result of this influence, Christians fell into a similar mindset toward physical things. They also misunderstood bodily resurrection, thinking the body held no value and would not be resurrected. This mindset led them to condone whatever physical actions they desired, believing the body would ultimately be destroyed. Paul's main goal in this text was to address the wrong thoughts about the body that lead the Corinthians to sin with the body. To change their behaviors, he had to first correct their thoughts.

Paul combated the Corinthians' sexually immoral lifestyles by commanding them to flee from those activities. But on a deeper level, he also sought to address their errant beliefs about the body because those beliefs drove their sinful behaviors. Paul carefully constructed two main points in these eight verses—that the body matters, and that God has authority over it. For the Corinthians to stop committing physical sins, they needed to know on a deeper level that their bodies, including what they did with them, were an important part of their faith.

Therefore, this is precisely why he mentioned the body so frequently to a group of Christians who thought the body was not valuable. It is this reality that gives us the perfect setting to build a biblical view of the body. Paul explained why the body mattered and how God has authority over it by connecting it with the Trinity.

By highlighting how the Father, Son, and Holy Spirit are involved with the body, he let the Corinthians know their thinking about the body was wrong. Likewise, they were not to do whatever they desired with their bodies. Paul's explanation serves as our foundation for thinking about and treating our bodies in ways that glorify God.

First, we will consider ten body statements from Paul in this passage. Then, we will use them to construct a framework for a God-honoring body image, one that sees the body as he does. Here are Paul's words in 1 Corinthians 6:12–20:

> "All things are lawful for me," but not all things are helpful. "All things are lawful for me," but I will not be dominated by anything. "Food is meant for the stomach and the stomach for food"—and God will destroy both one and the other. The body is not meant for sexual immorality, but for the Lord, and the Lord for the body. And God raised the Lord and will also raise us up by his power. Do you not know that your bodies are members of Christ? Shall I then take the members of Christ and make them members of a prostitute? Never! Or do you not know that he who is joined to a prostitute becomes one body with her? For, as it is written, "The two will become one flesh." But he who is joined to the Lord becomes one spirit with him. Flee from sexual immorality. Every other sin a person commits is outside the body, but the sexually immoral person sins against his own body. Or do you not know that your body

> is a temple of the Holy Spirit within you, whom you have from God? You are not your own, for you were bought with a price. So glorify God in your body.

In eight verses, Paul tells the Corinthian believers that:

1: Bodies are not meant to be enslaved to dominating passions (v. 12).
2: Bodies belong to the Lord (v. 13).
3: Bodies are meant for the Lord (v. 13).
4: Bodies will be raised (v. 14).
5: Bodies are members with Christ (v. 15).
6: Bodies are joined to the Lord (v. 17).
7: Bodies are temples of the Holy Spirit (v. 19).
8: Bodies are owned by God (v. 19).
9: Bodies are redeemed, along with our soul, by Christ's atonement (v. 20).
10: Bodies are instruments of glorifying God (v. 20).

From these ten, rapid-fire statements about the body in just eight verses, Paul's conviction that the body matters and that God has authority over it comes through loud and clear. The next time you are tempted to have destructive and negative thoughts about your body, go to Paul's statements. Take some time to carefully and slowly meditate on the principles we will discuss next that flow from these statements. Lies about your body do not stand a chance against such powerful truths.

In 1 Corinthians, Paul is writing to a church that didn't understand God's perspective on the body.

Instead, they thought it unimportant and thus gave into sinful, physical conduct. In similar ways, when we hold on to a negative body image and fail to see the body as God does, that can lead us to mistreat our bodies. But when armed with the truths of God's Word, Christians are supplied with powerful tools to overcome destructive body thoughts. Let's unpack some of the body image principles that can be drawn from 1 Corinthians 6:12–20.

Principle 1: A God-honoring body image declares the body's goodness because it bears God's image (v. 19).

One way we recognize that the body is the Lord's comes from creation. He formed humans as his very good, embodied image-bearers. We are the Lord's, not our own. In the Corinthians' decision to commit sexual sin, they not only denied the body's goodness but also marred God's image. Being made in God's image should inform everything done in the body, including how we think about and treat our bodies. To possess a body image that honors God, Christians must give up a body image that seeks to conform to worldly standards. Rather than viewing the body through worldly ideals, the body must be seen as inherently worthy because we bear God's image, which is also a sobering stamp of his ownership.

While God initially created his embodied image-bearers as his *very good* creation that was completely free from sin and corruption, we understand that the fall impacted every part of creation, including our bodies. But because the redemptive work of Christ secured the renewal of all creation, we await the redemption of our bodies (Romans 8:23). This promise means that Christians affirm the twin realities of sin's effect on our physical bodies and yet also the hope of perfected bodies in the new heavens and new earth (2 Peter 3:13). The body is a magnificent gift of God, and while presently marred by sin, it will one day become imperishable (1 Corinthians 15:51–54).

Principle 2: A God-honoring body image recognizes that the body is significant because it is connected to the Father, Son, and Holy Spirit (vv. 19–20).

Paul connects the body to each person of the Trinity to show the Corinthians that they are not their own and specifically that their bodies are not their own. By mentioning the divine works of resurrection (v. 14), redemption (v. 20), and indwelling (v. 19), Paul refers to these activities of the Father, Son, and Spirit as a way to confirm his point that the body matters, and God has authority over it. If the body does not matter, it will not be resurrected, it would not have been bought at the price of Christ's embodied life, and it would not serve as the dwelling place of the Spirit. But these realities are true, and thus, the body holds significance and value.

Principle 3: A God-honoring body image recognizes that the body is sacred (v. 19).

Because of the Holy Spirit's indwelling, Christians view their bodies as sacred. When Paul equated the Corinthians' bodies to the temple of the Holy Spirit, he communicated something profound. Because God's presence brings holiness and purity, wherever he dwells is sacred. Paul's declaration of the body as God's temple drastically opposed the Corinthians' poor conception of the body and unrestrained physical sin. Similarly, Christians cannot affirm the body's value as the Spirit's temple and at the same time harshly evaluate it from a negative body image. Likewise, the body cannot be mistreated to reach an outward ideal and also be respected as the dwelling place of the Holy Spirit. Recognizing the Spirit's indwelling helps Christians guard against any thinking, feeling, and acting that denigrates the temple God resides in.

Principle 4: A God-honoring body image acknowledges the body is for the Lord and dedicates it solely to him (v. 13).

The body is meant for the Lord and should not be devoted to other things. The Corinthians lived with the mindset that they could give themselves to whatever activities they chose. They did as they pleased, without any concern for how God might want them to view or use their bodies. But Paul told them the Lord is for their bodies, and their bodies are meant for him. Those struggling with negative body image must recognize that devotion to anything but the Lord is wrong.

Principle 5: A God-honoring body image submits to God's authority over the body (vv. 14–15, 19–20).

God displays his power and authority over the body in specific ways: through his ability to resurrect it, his power to purchase it with his blood, and the authority he holds by filling it with his presence. Negative body image views the body as seriously flawed. But when Christians recognize these powerful realities of God's authority, the way they see the body changes. We acknowledge our body's value because it is ultimately God's property, and he considers it valuable. So believers strive to surrender all bodily thoughts, feelings, and actions to God, who has claimed our body in such significant ways.

Principle 6: A God-honoring body image views the body as a member of Christ and treats it accordingly (v. 15).

Because our bodies are members of Christ's body, we must treat them as such, unlike the Corinthians, whose actions contradicted this truth. By their sinful choices, they committed two wrongs. First, they symbolically took their bodies from Christ and then joined them to prostitutes. Negative body image issues often create the same pattern. First, dissatisfaction with the body forgets its significance as a member with Christ. Then, that dissatisfaction fuels sinful choices. When the body is devalued in the mind, physical consequences result. Bodily displeasure may lead to acts of self-harm that damage the body, pushing past physical injuries through extreme exercise, willful vomiting from bulimia, chemically and surgically altering the body, or starving it as I did when I battled anorexia. But the Christian, whose body is a member of Christ, is called to treat that body with respect. This means making the hard choice to treat your body well, even when tempted to do otherwise.

Principle 7: A God-honoring body image understands union with Christ and the call to emulate his obedient embodied life (v. 17).

As Christians, we are united to Christ in salvation. To Paul, this union meant believers should recognize that their bodies are joined to the Lord, which comes with the expectation of Christlike conduct. We understand Christlikeness by reading about Christ's perfectly obedient, embodied life in the Gospels. So we dedicate ourselves to an obedient life, not one devoted to achieving a flawless appearance. Following Christ's example, we live to please the Father through our embodied existence, which our union with Christ enables.

Principle 8: A God-honoring body image seeks to intentionally glorify God in every aspect of embodied living (v. 20).

Paul's argument for the body's value and God's authority over it concludes with the command to glorify God in the body. Given the truths he listed about the body, now it is the Corinthians' turn to act. Everything done in the body is to be done for God's glory. Believing falsehoods about our physical form that drive negative emotions and lead to damaging actions will never bring God glory through the body.

Principle 9: A God-honoring body image fights wrong thoughts about the body (v. 20).

Acknowledging what God declares about our bodies also implies fighting wrong beliefs and thoughts. The Corinthians' errant beliefs about the body led them to sin, but Paul calls them to reject their false assumptions. For someone struggling with negative body image, denying the body's value or seeing it as defective and unattractive will fuel destructive thoughts and behaviors.

Principle 10: A God-honoring body image understands the strong temptation of worldly appearance standards and rejects giving into them (v. 12).

Paul implores the Corinthian believers to recognize that their misunderstanding of Christian freedom might lead to slavery instead. They were underestimating sin's power, acting like unbelievers, and were in danger of becoming enslaved to an ungodly lifestyle. Preoccupation with perceived physical flaws and obsession with meeting worldly appearance standards can enslave someone to negative body image. Sin issues like vanity and idolatry reinforce one another, making slaves of those who desire outward perfection. Because new areas of concern will always arise, the idolatrous quest for an acceptable body can be unending. If you are never satisfied with your appearance, the exhausting, enslaving cycle of negative body image will continue.

Principle 11: A God-honoring body image understands that if regular activities become controlling or harmful, they are sin (v. 12).

Freedom to live for Christ does not mean freedom to live for sin, an important point that Paul wanted the Corinthians to understand. Not only must we avoid outright sin but living for Christ may also mean avoiding actions that, while not inherently sinful, are ones that could end up mastering us and becoming sin. Sometimes negative body image can lead to actions that are not necessarily sinful, but if they control us or cause us to harm our bodies, they are wrong. Exercising, eating generous portions of rich food, or skipping a meal on occasion are not wrong. However, if these occasional choices become idolatrous obsessions, then they are not only sinful, but also harmful.

Principle 12: God-honoring body image is grateful for the divine ability to express self-control against worldly appearance desires and behaviors (v. 19).

As the Holy Spirit indwells believers, he imparts to them his fruit. One of them, the fruit of self-control, is essential in the fight against negative body image. Paul not only wanted the Corinthians to know that their body is the Spirit's temple, but also that the Spirit supplied them the divine ability to live a holy life. Only God could help them express the necessary self-control to flee sexual immorality. It is the same for us. The fruit of self-control provides the strength we need to battle critical thoughts and desires for a particular appearance. So when it comes to negative body image, being self-controlled means battling false and destructive beliefs about the body through the power of the Spirit. Only then can we find victory over such ingrained patterns of thinking, feeling, and acting.[2]

Principle 13: A God-honoring body image longs for the body's future restoration while wisely accepting the fact that the body will not be perfected in this age (v. 14).

Christians are to hope for the promised restoration of our body in resurrection rather than seeking bodily perfection now. The Corinthians did not believe in the resurrection, which led them to engage in sexual immorality. They thought the body had no future, so they devalued it and lived however they wanted in the present. But Paul confirmed the body's future in glorious resurrection. Only then will Christians have a perfect body, one that God will provide. Therefore, it is foolish to seek one now. The world says to pursue that perfect body while you can because without the right muscles, body shape, or abilities, you will never be good enough, which is why society pushes constant diets, plastic surgeries, and body-enhancing products. But believers must reject these expectations and be content with the knowledge that God will perfect the body at the resurrection.

Principle 14: A God-honoring body image knows the promise of resurrection and responds by thinking about and treating the body well (vv. 14–17).

Paul wanted the Corinthians to know that the future promise of bodily resurrection should impact their physical actions in the present. They were not to dishonor the bodies that God would one day honor in resurrection. Sinful bodily actions in the present are wrong because they reject the body's future glory. This recognition can motivate believers toward honorable thoughts about and treatment of the body. Just as the Corinthians were not to engage in sinful, physical activities like sexual immorality, so also we should not participate in physical actions like eating disorders, gluttony, bodily neglect, or anything else that causes physical damage. Damaging activities that arise from a negative body image dishonor the Lord because they afflict the body that he will one day resurrect.

One more factor in forming a God-honoring body image needs discussion. In the last section, we will consider how God specially readies his children to fight this battle against negative body image.

WE ARE UNIQUELY EQUIPPED TO COMBAT A NEGATIVE BODY IMAGE

Amazingly, Christians are uniquely equipped to combat negative body image. To close out this chapter on a biblical view of the body, we must reflect on how God supplies the necessary power we need to confront and correct thoughts of body displeasure. First, in Christ and through his divine power, he gives all Christians everything they need to live a godly life (2 Peter 1:3). Rather than relying on our own, feeble strength to battle negative thinking, he mercifully provides the perfect ability to display godliness in all areas of life. This includes our thoughts. Plus, as previously discussed, the Holy Spirit provides this power by indwelling believers, enabling us to be disciplined and self-controlled. By the Spirit, we are empowered to discipline our mind and body (Galatians 5:22–23). No longer beholden to the mind of the flesh, we possess the mind of Christ and the Holy Spirit, which entails the capacity to think thoughts that please God (Romans 8:5–6; 1 Corinthians 2:16).

This power over sin demonstrates that we can take thoughts captive that fail to obey Christ. When negative body thoughts arise, Christians claim them as lies, commit them to Christ, and choose truth. We can conform to Christ in our thoughts (2 Corinthians 10:4–6) and believers are commanded to set their minds on things above. This instruction implies we should not be consumed by things in the world, like chasing a fleeting appearance, beauty standard, or certain physique (Colossians 3:1–2). Instead, we seek godly thoughts and activities that are characterized as true, honorable, just, pure, lovely, commendable, excellent, and praiseworthy. After all, holding to such things serves as a powerful guard for our hearts and minds. When it comes to the destructive thoughts of negative body image, Philippians 4:8 reminds us to exchange such thoughts instead of entertaining them, which produces negative emotions and damaging actions. Simply put, because the mind directs our body image, Christians possess the unique ability to think, feel, and act toward the body in ways that honor God.

So be encouraged. Hopefully, this chapter has shown you that Christians can hold a body image that glorifies God. By knowing Scripture and understanding how it applies to the way we think, feel, and act, believers can learn to see their bodies as God does and overcome the struggle with negative body image.

REFLECTION QUESTIONS

1. In what ways does God's Word help you clarify what the world confuses about the body?

2. What verses can you memorize to meditate on when you battle negative body image?

3. In the fight against sin, how does it help us to remember that we possess divine power over our mind and body? How can we depend on God to provide this divine power?

4. Which truths did you find especially helpful for guarding against negative body image?

Chapter 6

HOW TO HONOR GOD IN THE BODY

Scripture shows us how to have a body image that honors God. When set in the context of typical body image issues, the framework from 1 Corinthians 6:12–20 can help to correct a negative body image in men and women of all ages. That process starts with listening to or reflecting on what led you to current distorted body thoughts. As you discern the cause(s), ask the Spirit to help you recognize, identify, and reject the lies you've believed about the body. Confession and repentance of those wrong thoughts are the next steps of healing. From there, you can make plans to address the influencing factors. Plans might involve using Scripture to counter the negative factors, beginning new habits, and behaviors, and learning to rely on the Spirit's help to resist the temptation to give in to negative body image cycles.

In this chapter, we will consider six scenarios that depict real-life body image concerns and see how the process to correct negative body image could happen for the following people: (1) Tate, a child with disabilities,

(2) Nora, a teenage girl, (3) Clay, a young adult, (4) Jackie, a postpartum mother, (5) Cynthia, a menopausal women, and (6) Thomas, a man in his midseventies. In each instance, I explain specific body image struggles and how a God-honoring body image reframes a negative one. These stories demonstrate how the previous principles can be applied in a variety of contexts but is not meant to simplify what could be a lifelong process of setbacks, growth, and victory over negative body image. These case studies are designed to exemplify a process that may not always be straightforward and easy. Because Christians progress in sanctification throughout their entire lives, we press on to pursue a God-honoring body image by the power of the Spirit toward maturity in Christ.

TATE—A CHILD WITH DISABILITIES

A Christian body image must address disability, as body image issues are not limited to those who feel fat, hate their long arms, or want more muscle definition. A child born with physical disabilities experiences the world differently from other family members. From a young age, Tate's parents taught him that his physical differences did not need to limit him. But, as he grows, he cannot help but ask God: *Why is my body different? Did I do something wrong? Does God not love me like he does those with a normal body?* Slowed by physical inabilities, Tate wishes to run around with his siblings and friends. Unlike his siblings, his mom still bathes and dresses him. He must depend on others to meet his needs; his freedom is limited to their availability.

But within Tate's disability is a heightened ability to grasp the depth of grace God offers in the gospel. Though his body is impacted by sin like all of creation, he can have a deeper appreciation than most for the promise of bodily resurrection. Tate can learn that God lovingly cares for and holds power over all creation, even the parts of his body that operate differently from others. Though his disability is a result of the fall, Tate knows he is made in God's image, body and soul (Principle 1). His physical form was not an accident but intricately shaped and knitted together just as God saw fit. So Tate recognizes that God is not pleased when he thinks ugly or mean things about his body. He also comes to realize that comparing his body to siblings or friends is not what God wants him to do and asks for help to trust God's purpose for designing his differently-abled body. His parents help Tate make a plan to regularly read the Gospels, which comfort him with the knowledge that Jesus heals disabilities. He trusts that this will not always be the condition of his body. He recognizes that Christ cared especially for those with disabilities and that he loved him so much that he took on a body in order to save him from his sins. Tate reads about how Christ also experienced physical suffering; this knowledge helps him remember that Jesus has deep sympathy for the pain he feels on a regular basis (Principle 2). Despite his disabilities, with childlike faith, he commits to sharing with others how much God loves him and all that he has done for him.[1]

NORA—A TEENAGE GIRL

Teenage years can be especially distressing for teen girls whose bodies might have changed earlier or later than their friends' bodies and who feel pressure to fit in. In these years, teens often seek conformity to whatever is considered attractive, popular, or desirable. Nora faces these pressures, especially as she hopes to be a cheerleader for her school football team. She often compares her body to the other girls and frequently engages in negative self-talk about her perceived flaws. Her thoughts are often filled with questions: *What do others think about the shape of my hips? Did I suck my stomach in enough on the video that was just posted? Should I start saving money to get plastic surgery in a few years?*

Still, a body image that glorifies God is possible for Nora by recognizing that she should believe and listen to what Scripture says about her body. God's Word describes her physical form as his wondrous work that he lovingly fashioned in her mother's womb. This understanding can correct the negative self-talk she is tempted to engage in. Nora's body was a beautifully made gift by her loving Father, who gives her life and breath, so it is valuable and significant. It is not an undesirable thing to be hated. Being aware of the temptation to fit in, she refuses to skip meals, starve her body, or regularly purge like others, recognizing that believers ought not harm their bodies in such worldly ways (Principle 10). Confessing her desire to conform to the beauty standards of the world, Nora chooses to limit the influence of those who drastically cut calories to lose weight. She especially feels this influence on social media, so she unfollows accounts and stops making posts that tempt her to define her worth by the number of likes she gets.

She regularly reminds herself that her body is for the Lord to combat negative thoughts. She knows thinking rightly about her body honors the Lord, which also means not seeking to please others with her looks or engaging in disordered behaviors just to fit in. Because God owns her body, she knows mistreating it for her self-focused goals are wrong. She determines to fight destructive body thoughts because she would not think such things about the Lord (Principle 9). Because her body is united to him, she learns how to respectfully care for it. Grateful for the indwelling Holy Spirit, she asks for his help to fight the lies about her body, knowing these thoughts only depress and lead her toward sin and harmful behaviors. By relying on the Spirit's power to guard her mind, Nora learns to discern the difference between falsehood and truth.

CLAY—A YOUNG ADULT

Navigating the challenges of college life, like coursework, new friends, a job, or the potential of dating, is a lot for a young adult. Moreover, the pressure is constant to achieve a certain physical form to build muscle and fit the mold of what the world says is attractive. Clay desires to be friends with the guys who hang out in the gym but also realizes they seem obsessed about their image on social media. Rather than turning to worldly efforts to improve his body, Clay must realize that worldly messages for how to improve his body only seek to fulfill temporal desires. Desires for a better-looking appearance are only aimed at pleasing himself and living up to the expectations of others. Plus, those worldly messages and desires can cause him to wonder: *Do I spend enough hours in the gym? Should I try taking steroids? If I fail to have a certain physique, will girls ever be interested in me?* In this challenging stage of life, it is important to let Scripture, not society, define his worth.

Surrounded by the pressure to appeal to girls and a culture that fuels comparison, Clay can rest in knowing that his muscle mass and height are inconsequential to his character. He admits that chasing worldly appearance goals can produce poor character and unwise choices, which he has seen in his peers. He learns from their mistakes, while refusing to be consumed by the drive to unwisely enhance his body. He knows that those obsessive thoughts are idolatrous and will only lead to destructive actions. He also recalls that he should devote his body to the Lord, not to things that promise temporal satisfaction with hollow results (Principle 4). Excessive, lengthy gym workouts combined with an endless pursuit of products to enhance his body can threaten his devotion to the Lord. With this recognition, Clay evaluates the motivations of his heart. From this heart posture, he confesses the times of idolizing his body by prioritizing it over spiritual things. Instead, he chooses to steward his body in ways that honor God through moderate activity and rest.

Ultimately, God holds final authority over his body, which Clay remembers when tempted with dissatisfaction over his appearance. Unlike many his age, he fights the consuming lifestyle of conforming to the societal ideal. He sees the futility in that lifestyle, which requires countless hours of exercise, wasted time scrolling social media for workout tips, and following strict eating regimens. Though Clay wants a fit physique, he works to rely on the Holy Spirit's fruit of self-control when faced with daunting desires for an ideal body type (Principle 12). Fighting for a disciplined thought life, the young adult male refuses to define his value by comparing himself with others.

JACKIE—A POSTPARTUM MOM

Over the course of her pregnancy, a mother's body endures many changes as she prepares to support, nourish, and protect another human being. Some of these "physiognomical and psychosocial changes" include "hormonal fluctuations, the experience of pregnancy-related physical symptoms and changes to appearance (e.g., nausea, backache, varicose veins, stretch marks, acne, and swollen ankles and feet), changes to one's interactions and relationships with others, and the adaptation to being a new mother."[2] Given societal pressures, new mom Jackie feels overwhelmed by the physical differences in her postpartum body. Finding them difficult to accept, she feels worries: *Does my husband find me undesirable? What if the weight never decreases on my face? Will I ever be able to find a bathing suit that hides these new stretch marks?* These bodily changes coupled with shifting emotions impact her body image in negative ways, especially because she was dissatisfied with her body prior to pregnancy. Plus, her body is still carrying excess weight from pregnancy.

Jackie determines to agree with God's Word when she assesses her physical form as wonderfully created in God's image and praises him for it. She grows in humility as she is grateful that God specially designed and fitted her body with the ability to carry children. Jackie's postpartum form is not what makes her valuable because Christ unconditionally accepts and loves her, despite the changes in her appearance after pregnancy. She repents of despairing over her body and prays for help to process these changes with sober judgment. Instead of focusing on these "flaws," Jackie sees them as humble reminders of her newborn. She fights to surrender idealistic expectations when they lead to dissatisfaction over new body marks and shapes. Realizing the futility of comparing herself to other moms is not wise or helpful, she guards against fueling the negativity, worry, and insecurity that often arise from looking at social media.

Jackie knows she will need the Holy Spirit's power to keep her thoughts disciplined when disappointed in her appearance. Grateful for the Spirit's consistent faithfulness, Jackie trusts him, even when she waivers. Admittedly, she faces the temptation to lean on extreme health fads and diets to lose the baby weight. Still, she understands these drastic measures could harm her health and are not wise ways to steward her body. Making reasonable eating and exercise choices, Jackie remembers her body is a member of Christ's and strives to treat it well (Principle 6). Because Christians are to glorify God with their bodies, she confesses the destructive patterns of thought that revolve around her body (Principle 8). Negatively assessing her appearance and fixating on her perceived flaws directly oppose thinking about her body in ways that bring God glory. Jackie cannot honor him for his wondrous works while simultaneously rejecting the goodness of her body. Nor should she endeavor to perfect her body now when it is God who will perfect it in resurrection (Principle 13). As each person of the Trinity—Father, Son, and Holy Spirit—affirm her physical existence, she comprehends the added significance of carrying another image-bearer. Such reminders help Jackie focus on cultivating a body image that is based on Scripture while also giving thanks to the Lord for her body's incredible abilities.

CYNTHIA—A MENOPAUSAL WOMAN

In older adulthood, for men and women alike, body concerns should focus on preparing the mind and body for old age by guarding against the effects of aging. Adults need to work on balance and coordination since these skills decrease with age and, as a result, increase the likelihood of falls and injuries. Also, instead of exercising to achieve an ideal body, there should be a mindset shift of exercising to improve overall health, as incidences of diabetes, high cholesterol, high blood pressure, and other chronic diseases increase with age. Altering a negative body image is more effective when functional, physical health is prioritized.

Seemingly at every age, women battle negative body images, but the additional physical and emotional strain of menopause can cause even greater anguish and distress over the body. A menopausal woman often gains weight that collects around her midsection due to fluctuating hormones, a major reason why studies reveal a negative shift in body image from a woman's premenopausal body to postmenopausal body.[3] Though the natural effects of menopause can lead to increased weight, Cynthia finds herself disparaging her body because of it. She has started to despair over questions like: *Will I be able to get this weight off? Why do I feel like my body has less value because of these changes? Should I start skipping meals?*

While believers may temporarily lament this challenging transition, ultimately, they seek refuge in biblical truths that support a body image that honors God. Not only should Cynthia recall that God created her, but he also designed her body to experience the physical effects of menopause. Because of that reality, there is no reason to entertain feelings of shame. She asks God for forgiveness knowing that he isn't honored when she judges herself for the menopausal changes. As Cynthia desires to glorify God with her body during menopause, she submits to his authority over her body, marked by this once-in-a-lifetime season (Principle 5). Her Father lovingly intended this unique occurrence to be part of her embodied experience as a woman. And he has providentially sustained and guided her life into this new season, one that she seeks to accept with gratitude.

Despite the desire to restrict calories and workout excessively to address unwanted weight gain, Cynthia refuses to give in. She fights the discontentment, not allowing that potential harm to her body. Plus, those activities could likely enslave her, causing her to idolize her physical shape (Principle 11). Cynthia's temporary physical changes bring reminders of permanent bodily completeness that God will one day accomplish. To seek a perfect exterior now is to pursue vanity and fall into the continuous trap of living to meet worldly ideals. By the Spirit's presence in her, Cynthia's body is sacred precisely as it is now, so she fights negativity and fault-finding (Principle 3). With these choices, she determines to glorify God and pursue Christlikeness in her menopausal body by thinking about and treating it in honorable ways.

THOMAS—A MAN IN HIS MIDSEVENTIES

Even though our bodies stop growing, they continue to change due to aging throughout adult life.[4] With changes come disappointment, pain, and limitation, all of which create mental anguish that undoubtedly influences body image. Knowing how his body used to function, the steps he once climbed with ease, and the good hearing or memory he once had, the aging male has become dejected with the state of his failing body. Questions flood his mind: *With my back pain, how long will I be able to continue working outdoors? Am I eventually going to need a hearing aid or a walker to get around? How will arthritis affect the hobbies I love so much?* Burdened by questions with unknown answers, Thomas begins to hate his body for the first time in his life.

To combat this mindset, Thomas reminds himself to look to God to define this new phase in life, finding his identity in his union with Christ. He regrets and repents of spending so much time lamenting his changing, aging body and thanks the Lord that his body remains God's remarkable creation. Tolerating despairing thoughts over his body's former abilities is not only a waste of time but also takes away his ability to enjoy his current season of life. He knows exercise will benefit him as he ages, whereas being idle will speed up the aging process.

With this mindset, Thomas relies on the grace to accept his body as it is now, devoting his physical abilities to the Lord. Practically caring for his body shows that he still values it and has not allowed his declining abilities to lead him to give up. And as an embodied being, he realizes that downcast or dreadful thoughts will also impact him spiritually.

Despite his physical weakening, Thomas trusts in God's promise to resurrect and complete his adoption in the redemption of his body (Romans 8:23). This trust in a perfected, glorified body brings a longing for an existence without limitation and pain. He rejoices in these truths and fights to center his mind on them when tempted toward a negative body image (Principle 14). On these occasions, he praises God while longing for an eternity where his body will no longer deteriorate or fail. He recognizes that his body's decline is within God's sovereign control. As he trusts that his loving Father will not forsake him when his strength is spent, Thomas's faith grows in grateful, humble dependence. Rather than finding his comfort and identity in what he can do physically, he places it in Christ and strives to imitate his embodied obedience to the Father (Principle 7). Paul's words of outwardly wasting away yet inwardly being renewed ring truer now more than ever (2 Corinthians 4:16). So he chooses to trust what the Lord has for him now and prays for a refreshed motivation to glorify God in his body—even through old age, gray hairs, and potential physical inabilities.[5]

REFLECTION QUESTIONS

1. Which of the stories shared in this chapter was the most relatable to you? How will that story impact the way you think about or act toward your body?

2. Did you recognize any of your friends in the people described in this chapter? What is one truth you might share with your friends to help them grow in thinking about their body as God thinks about it?

3. What are some specific ways you can honor God in your body, as it is right now?

4. Are there any Bible verses you read in this chapter that speak to your struggles? If so, memorize it, meditate on it, and consider if there are any actions God is prompting you to take.

CONCLUSION

Christians face an onslaught of temptations from the world, the devil, and even our own flesh to believe lies about the body that produce destructive emotions and lead to actions of bodily harm. This pattern happens when we run our view of the body through a subjective framework that we define for ourselves from worldly influences. The outcome is a judgment call on whether our body measures up to our expectations. And when it fails to, we are often compelled to "fix" the focal issues at any cost. But it does not have to be that way.

In Christ, believers are supplied with grace and strength for today, in whatever battles we face. So we hold fast to the gospel message, that Christ has taken the penalty for our sins and given us his righteousness and ultimate victory over all forms of sin. As we look to Christ, turning our minds to him and away from the world, we will progressively learn what it means to think God's thoughts about our bodies. Then, supplied with all we need for life and godliness, we can act in ways that honor him, participate in the divine nature, and escape corruption caused by the world and evil desires (2 Peter 1:3–8).

Because of the divine power given to us in the gospel, Christians can strive to switch out that middle filter, our subjective framework, for an objective one built on God's Word. This striving to think biblically about our bodies will be a process, just as the battle against any sinful pattern takes time and intentional effort. But as we seek to know God's Word, confess lies, receive forgiveness, renew our minds with truth, and rely on the Holy Spirit's power to work in us, our body image will change.

In the end, Christians should rejoice, as the Bible contains all we need to battle negative body image. We need not look to therapeutical methods or cultural movements to correct our thoughts and soothe our minds, although we can learn some helpful strategies from them due to God's common grace. The world cannot offer any lasting fixes through plastic surgery or the latest social media fad. In the struggle against negative body image, if we really desire a God-honoring body image, we must prioritize believing what he says rather than entertaining outside influences. Know his Word, and trust his help to exchange your thoughts for his truths. Then, act on those truths to glorify God in your body. Switching out your subjective framework for a biblical one will take time, but God has powerfully equipped you. Believe what he says, think his truths, and see your body as he sees it.

ENDNOTES

Chapter 1

1. Linda Smolak, "Body Image Development in Childhood," in *Body Image: A Handbook of Science, Practice, and Prevention, in Body Image: A Handbook of Theory, Research, and Clinical Practice*, ed. Thomas F. Cash and Linda Smolak, 2nd ed. (New York: Guilford Press, 2011), 68–74.

2. "About Obesity," Centers for Disease Control and Prevention, January 23, 2024, https://www.cdc.gov/obesity/php/about/index.html.

3. Smolak, "Body Image Development in Childhood," 69.

4. "How Social Media Affects Body Image," https://socialmediavictims.org/mental-health/body-image/.

5. Heather R. Gallivan, "Teens, Social Media, and Body Image," https://pdf4pro.com/fullscreen/teens-social-media-and-body-image-macmh-9cd17.html.

6. Smolak, "Body Image Development in Childhood," 71.

7. Alexandra Dane and Komal Bhatia, "Social Media Diet: A Scoping Review of the Association Between Social Media, Body Image, and Eating Disorders Amongst Young People," March 22, 2023, https://journals.plos.org/globalpublichealth/article?id=10.1371/journal.pgph.0001091.

8. "Body Image in Children 2-8 Years," https://raisingchildren.net.au/school-age/health-daily-care/mental-health/body-image-children-2-8-years.

9. "Social Media and Youth Mental Health", https://www.hhs.gov/surgeongeneral/priorities/youth-mental-health/social-media/index.html.

10. David Bickham, Elizabeth Hunt, Benoit Bediou, and Michael Rich, "Adolescent Media Use: Attitudes, Effects, and Online Expectations" (Boston, MA: Boston Children's Hospital Digital Wellness Lab, 2022) https://digitalwellnesslab.org/wp-content/uploads/Pulse-Survey_Adolescent-Attitudes-Effects-and-Experiences.pdf.

11. Heather Gallivan, "Teens, Social Media, and Body Image," https://pdf4pro.com/fullscreen/teens-social-media-and-body-image-macmh-9cd17.html.

12. Sarah Grogan, "Body Image Development in Adulthood," in *Body Image*, 97.

13. Gallivan, "Teens, Social Media, and Body Image."

14. S. Daniel and S. K. Bridges, "The relationships among body image, masculinity, and sexual satisfaction in men," *Psychology of Men & Masculinity* 14, no. 4 (2013): 345–51. https://doi.org/10.1037/a0029154.

15. Grogan, "Body Image Development in Adulthood," 96.

16. Grogan, 96.

Chapter 2

1. *Diagnostic and Statistical Manual of Mental Disorders: DSM-5*, 5th ed. (Washington, DC: American Psychiatric Association, 2013), 243.

2. Katherine A. Phillips, "Body Image and Body Dysmorphic Disorder," in *Body Image: A Handbook of Theory, Research, and Clinical Practice*, ed. Thomas F. Cash and Linda Smolak, 2nd ed. (New York: Guilford Press, 2011), 305–6.

3. *DSM-5*, 244.

4. Lainey Greer, "The Utilization of the Theology of the Body to Address Body Image" (PhD diss., Southern Baptist

Theological Seminary, 2021), 105–8, https://repository.sbts.edu/bitstream/handle/10392/6643/Greer_sbts_0207D_10687.pdf?sequence=1&isAllowed=y.

5. Philipps, "Body Image and Body Dysmorphic Disorder," in *Body Image*, 311.

6. Victoria Hoff and Olivia Hancock, "Society's 'Ideal' Female Body Type," updated January 24, 2024. Retrieved from https://www.byrdie.com/body-standards-survey.

7. Marika Tiggemann, "Human Appearance and Body Image," in *Body Image*, 16.

8. Eleanor H. Wertheim and Susan J. Paxton, "Body Image Development in Adolescent Girls," in *Body Image*, 80.

9. "Social Media and Youth Mental Health," https://www.hhs.gov/surgeongeneral/priorities/youth-mental-health/social-media/index.html.

10. Georgia Wells, Jeff Horwitz, and Deepa Seetharaman, "Facebook Knows Instagram Is Toxic for Teen Girls, Company Documents Show," *Wall-Street Journal*, September 14, 2021, https://www.wsj.com/articles/facebook-knows-instagram-is-toxic-for-teen-girls-company-documents-show-11631620739.

11. Allyson Chiu, "Patients Are Desperate to Resemble Their Doctored Selfies. Plastic Surgeons Alarmed by 'Snapchat Dysphoria,'" *Washington Post*, August 6, 2018, https://www.washingtonpost.com/news/morning-mix/wp/2018/08/06/patients-are-desperate-to-resemble-their-doctored-selfies-plastic-surgeons-alarmed-by-snapchat-dysmorphia/.

12. "Surgeon General Issues New Advisory about Effects Social Media Use Has on Youth Mental Health," US Department of Health and Human Services, May 23, 2023, https://www.hhs.gov/about/news/2023/05/23/surgeon-general-issues-new-advisory-about-effects-social-media-use-has-youth-mental-health.html.

13. Chris Palmer, "In Brief: Limiting Social Media Boosts Mental Health, the Negatives of Body Positivity, and More Research," *Monitor on Psychology* 54, no. 8 (November/December 2023), https://www.apa.org/monitor/2023/11/benefits-limiting-social-media.

14. K. E. Riehm, K. A. Feder, and K. N. Tormohlen, "Associations Between Time Spent Using Social Media and Internalizing and Externalizing Problems Among US Youth," *JAMA Psychiatry* 76, no. 12 (2019): 1266–73. doi:10.1001/jamapsychiatry.2019.2325.

15. "Health Advisory on Social Media Use in Adolescence," American Psychological Association (May 2023), https://www.apa.org/topics/social-media-internet/health-advisory-adolescent-social-media-use.

16. "Health Advisory on Social Media Use in Adolescence."

17. "Health Advisory on Social Media Use in Adolescence."

18. Lina A. Ricciardelli and Marita P. McCabe, "Body Image Development in Adolescent Boys," in *Body Image*, 81–87.

19. Thomas F. Cash, "Cognitive-Behavioral Perspectives on Body Image," in *Body Image*, 40–42.

20. Cash, "Cognitive-Behavioral Perspectives on Body Image," 44.

21. Stacey Tantleff-Dunn and Danielle M. Lindner, "Body Image and Social Functioning," in *Body Image*, 263.

22. Nita Mary McKinley, "Feminist Perspectives on Body Image in *Body Image*, 49.

23. Rena Goldman, "The Stages of Puberty: Development in Boys and Girls," *Healthline*, August 23, 2018, https://www.healthline.com/health/parenting/stages-of-puberty#tanner-stage-2.

24. Ricciardelli and McCabe, "Body Image Development in Adolescent Boys," 87.

25. Luke Timothy Johnson, *The Revelatory Body: Theology as Inductive Art* (Grand Rapids: Eerdmans, 2015), 206.

26. Johnson, *The Revelatory Body*, 210–11.

27. Johnson, *The Revelatory Body*, 212.

28. Greer, "The Utilization of the Theology of the Body," 195.

29. Eleanor H. Wertheim and Susan J. Paxton, "Body Image Development in Adolescent Girls," in *Body Image*, 77.

30. Donald R. McCreary, "Body Image and Muscularity," in *Body Image*, 198.

31. Ricciardelli and McCabe, "Body Image Development in Adolescent Boys," 85.

Chapter 3

1. "Eating Disorder Statistics," The Checkup, January 24, 2024, https://www.singlecare.com/blog/news/eating-disorder-statistics/.

2. *DSM-5*, 338.

3. Janis H. Crowther and Nicole M. Williams, "Body Image and Bulimia Nervosa," in *Body Image: A Handbook of Theory, Research, and Clinical Practice*, ed. Thomas F. Cash and Linda Smolak, 2nd ed. (New York: Guilford Press, 2011), 289.

4. "Fast Facts on Eating Disorders," Academy for Eating Disorders, https://www.aedweb.org/aedold/resources/resources/fast-facts.

5. Rebecca Fuller and Kathleen Peterson, "Anorexia Nervosa in Adolescents," *Nursing 2020* 49, no. 10 (October 2019): 26.

6. Fuller and Peterson, "Anorexia Nervosa in Adolescents," 25.

7. "Eating Disorders and Males," https://nedc.com.au/eating-disorders/eating-disorders-explained/eating-disorders-in-males.

8. Laura Hurd Clarke, "Older Women and the Embodied Experience with Weight," in Hillary L. McBride and Janelle L. Kwee, eds., *Embodiment and Eating Disorders* (New York: Routledge, 2018), 191.

9. Sherrie Selwyn Delinsky, "Body Image and Anorexia Nervosa," in *Body Image*, 280.

10. Sherrie Selwyn Delinsky, "Body Image and Anorexia Nervosa," in *Body Image*, 280.

11. *DSM-5*, 342.

12. Patricia Westmoreland, Mori J. Krantz, and Philip S. Mehler, "Medical Complications of Anorexia Nervosa and Bulimia Nervosa," *American Journal of Medicine* 129, no. 1 (July 2015): 30–37.

13. Westmoreland, Krantz, and Mehler, "Anorexia Nervosa and Bulimia Nervosa."

14. Lainey Greer, "The Utilization of the Theology of the Body to Address Body Image" (PhD diss., Southern Baptist Theological Seminary, 2021), 101–3.

15. Janis H. Crowther and Nicole M. Williams, "Body Image and Bulimia Nervosa," in *Body Image*, 282.

16. *DSM-5*, 345.

17. Crowther and Williams, "Body Image and Bulimia Nervosa," 292.

18. Crowther and Williams, "Body Image and Bulimia Nervosa," 292.

19. *DSM-5*, 345.

20. Joshua I. Hrabosky, "Body Image and Binge-Eating Disorder," in *Body Image*, 296.

21. Hrabosky, "Body Image and Binge-Eating Disorder," 296.

22. "Binge Eating Disorder," National Eating Disorders Association, accessed January 18, 2024, https://www.nationaleatingdisorders.org/binge-eating-disorder/.

23. "What Are Eating Disorders?," American Psychiatric Association, reviewed February 2023, https://www.psychiatry.org/patients-families/eating-disorders/what-are-eating-disorders#section_3.

24. "The Rise of Muscle Dysmorphia," Butterfly, March 22, 2021, https://butterfly.org.au/the-rise-of-muscle-dysmorphia/.

25. Peter Flax, "'Bigorexia' Has Young Men Doing Dangerous Things for Muscle," *Men's Health*, September 19, 2022, https://www.menshealth.com/fitness/a41133394/bigorexia-muscle-dysmorphia-special-report/.

26. David Ludden, "What Is Rapid Onset Gender Dysphoria?," *Psychology Today*, May 4, 2023, https://www.psychologytoday.com/us/blog/talking-apes/202304/what-is-rapid-onset-gender-dysphoria.

27. Ludden, "What Is Rapid Onset Gender Dysphoria?"

28. Lisa Marchiano, "Outbreak: On Transgender Teens and Psychic Epidemics," *Psychological Perspectives* 60, no. 3 (2017): 345–66, https://www.tandfonline.com/doi/full/10.1080/00332925.2017.1350804.

29. "What Is Gender Dysphoria?," American Psychiatric Association, reviewed August 2022, https://www.psychiatry.org/patients-families/gender-dysphoria/what-is-gender-dysphoria.

Chapter 4

1. Melissa Rudy, "Top Plastic Surgery Procedures," Fox News, October 12, 2023, https://www.foxnews.com/health/top-plastic-surgeries-these-were-most-demand-procedures-2022.

2. N. Khunger, "Complications in Cosmetic Surgery: A Time to Reflect and Review and Not Sweep Them Under the Carpet," *J Cutan Aesthet Surg* 8, no. 4 (October–December 2015): 189–90. doi: 10.4103/0974-2077.172188. PMID: 26865782; PMCID: PMC4728899.

3. E. H. Aktas, U. D. Balci, and E. Karacaoglu, "COVID Pandemic Aftermath: Changing Dynamics on Cosmetic and Aesthetic Surgery Demands," Aesthetic Plastic Surgery 47, no. 4 (August 2023): 1658–65. doi: 10.1007/s00266-022-03231-9. Epub 2023 Jan 30. PMID: 36715726; PMCID: PMC9886203.

4. "'TikTok Face' Impact on Plastic Surgery," American Academy of Facial Plastic and Reconstructive Surgery, https://www.aafprs.org/Media/Press_Releases/%E2%80%98TikTok-Face%E2%80%99-Impact-On-Facial-Plastic-Surgery.aspx?WebsiteKey=5d3e122f-6cba-47ca-a903-c75cb1c94f61.

5. Lechia Bushak, "Selfies, Social Media Driving Up Rates of Cosmetic Surgeries Among Young People," August 25, 2023, https://www.mmm-online.com/home/channel/selfies-social-media-driving-up-rates-of-cosmetic-surgeries-among-young-people/.

6. Dana Magee, "Positive Body Image vs Body Positivity," Rebecca Bitzer and Associates, last updated September 16, 2021, https://rbitzer.com/positive-body-image-vs-body-positivity/; Kristen Fuller, "Body Positivity vs Body Neutrality," Very Well Mind, June 30, 2022, https://www.verywellmind.com/body-positivity-vs-body-neutrality-5184565.

7. Suseth Mena, "Why the Fat Acceptance Movement Is a Public Health Issue," *The Reporter*, October 18, 2019, https://mdcthereporter.com/why-the-fat-acceptance-movement-is-a-public-health-issue/.

8. Thomas F. Cash, "Cognitive-Behavioral Perspectives on Body Image," in *Body Image: A Handbook of Theory, Research, and Clinical Practice*, ed. Thomas F. Cash and Linda Smolak, 2nd ed. (New York: Guilford Press, 2011), 39.

9. Marika Tiggemann, "Human Appearance and Body Image," in *Body Image*, 13.

10. Lainey Greer, "The Utilization of the Theology of the Body to Address Body Image" (PhD diss., Southern Baptist Theological Seminary, 2021), 93.

Chapter 5

1. "Adult Obesity Prevalence Maps," Centers for Disease Control and Prevention, last modified March 31, 2021, https://www.cdc.gov/obesity/data/prevalence-maps.html; "Most Religious States 2021," World Population Review, https://worldpopulationreview.com/en/state-rankings/most-religious-states.

2. Lainey Greer, "The Utilization of the Theology of the Body to Address Body Image" (PhD diss., Southern Baptist Theological Seminary, 2021), 168–75.

Chapter 6

1. Greer, Lainey Greer, "The Utilization of the Theology of the Body to Address Body Image" (PhD diss., Southern Baptist Theological Seminary, 2021), 177–81.

2. Helen Skouteris, "Body Image Issues in Obstetrics and Gynecology," in *Body Image: A Handbook of Theory, Research, and Clinical Practice*, ed. Thomas F. Cash and Linda Smolak, 2nd ed. (New York: Guilford Press, 2011), 342.

3. Skouteris, "Body Image Issues in Obstetrics and Gynecology," 346.

4. Karyn M. Skultety and Susan Krauss Whitbourne, "Body Image Development Adulthood and Aging," in *Body Image*, 83.

5. Greer, "The Utilization of the Theology of the Body," 177–97.